HERITAGE WALKS
in
PEMBROKESHIRE

John Fenna

Copyright © John Fenna, 1997

Published by Sigma Leisure – an imprint of
Sigma Press, 1 South Oak Lane, Wilmslow, Cheshire SK9 6AR, England.

British Library Cataloguing in Publication Data
A CIP record for this book is available from the British Library.

ISBN: 1-85058-574-1

Typesetting and Design by: Sigma Press, Wilmslow, Cheshire.

Cover photograph: Above Whitesands Bay (John Fenna)

Text photographs: John Fenna

Maps: Jeremy Semmens

Printed by: MFP Design & Print

Disclaimer: the information in this book is given in good faith and is believed to be correct at the time of publication. No responsibility is accepted by either the author or publisher for errors or omissions, or for any loss or injury howsoever caused. Only you can judge your own fitness, competence and experience.

Preface

I hope that this collection of walks leads to visitors and locals enjoying the superb scenery of North Pembrokeshire from the healthiest, cheapest and – to me at least – the most pleasurable method of transport – walking on your own two feet.

I would like to thank everyone who helped me in producing this book especially the following:

The Ordnance Survey – especially Steven Yates – without whose maps the walks could not have been attempted; Tom Goodall, the Pembrokeshire Coast National Park's Access Officer and President of the Dyfed Area of The Ramblers' Association; Anthony Richards, of Dyfed County Council Planning Department; Jeremy George, Solicitor and Steward to the Barony of Kemes; Jonathon Hughes and Richard Ellis, National Trust Head Wardens, who all checked that the routes described were not going to cause any problems and corrected small errors in the draft of this book as well as giving additional information; Hazel Jones for reading (and correcting) the typescript and proofs.

Last, but far from least, my wife Lis, who has not only typed most of this work but generally does all my typing, correcting, accounts, cooking, cleaning, gardening, ironing, photocopying etc as well as holding down a full time job! I occasionally let her have time off to carry the rucksack on walks with me as well.

This book has been compiled in accordance with the "Guidelines for Writers of Path Guides" produced by the Outdoor Writer's Guild.

John Fenna

Contents

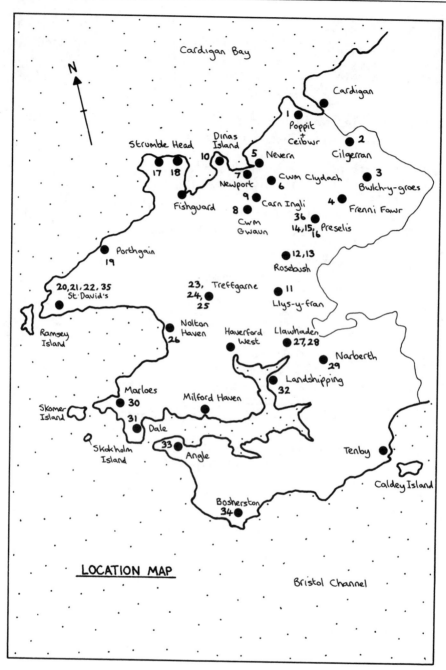

Cardigan Bay

N

Cardigan

Strumble Head

Dinas
Island

1
Poppit
+
Ceibwr

2
Cilgerran

10

5 Nevern

17 18

7

Cwm Clydach
6

3
Bwlch-y-groes

Newport

9

Carn Ingli

4
Frenni Fawr

Fishguard

8

36

Cwm
Gwaun

14,15,
16

Preselis

Porthgain

12,13

19

Rosebush

20,21,22,35
St David's

23,
24,
25

Treffgarne

11

Llys-y-fran

Ramsey
Island

Nolton
Haven

26

Haverford
West

Llawhaden

27,28

29

Narberth

Skomer
Island

Marloes

30

31

Dale

Milford Haven

Landshipping

32

Skokholm
Island

33

Angle

Tenby

Caldey Island

LOCATION MAP

Bosherston

34

Bristol Channel

Introduction

The North Pembrokeshire countryside and coastline offers a variety of scenery from sand dunes and towering sea cliffs to moorland and crags, rolling farmland and deep wooded valleys to river gorges and tidal marshes. All of these various landscapes offer superb walking and the choice of different types of scenery in a small area.

Most of the high ground is made up of hard Ordovician volcanic rocks, the lowlands are Ordovician sedimentaries while Cambrian and pre-Cambrian rocks are to be found around Hayscastle and St David's.

Man has left his mark on the landscape in a variety of ways with prehistoric features such as cairns, cromlechs and hill forts, standing stones and hut circles being found in abundance. The Preseli Hills are famous as the source of the Stonehenge Bluestones, and ancient legends tell of King Arthur, Celtic saints and giants all being active in the area. More recent signs of man's influence on the area are Roman, Celtic and Norman remains as well as disused quarries, old railway lines and old "green roads", while the rural landscape has been totally formed by changing farm practices.

Pembrokeshire is famous for its wealth of wild flowers and plants, some of them rare. The wide variety of environments means a wide variety of species and at most times of the year you can find many of these in flower, while spring is a riot of colour and in autumn the hills are ablaze with the combined glory of gorse and heather.

This wide range of habitats also gives great variety to the bird life. The coast is naturally a haven for sea birds, including the clown-like puffin, while various birds of prey, notably the buzzard, but also kestrels, peregrines and others will be seen patrolling the hills.

Mammals are also seen in great variety from dolphins and seals in the bays, seal pups a charming addition to the rocky coves when new born and nearly helpless, while signs of badgers and foxes are seen in most parts. On the hills you will find many roaming ponies and sheep, while Welsh Black cattle will be found on many farms.

When out walking, I recommend that you carry field guides to bird, mammal and plant life (Collins 'Gem' Books are excellent) and a pair of binoculars to help identify the wildlife and flowers.

About the Walks

The appropriate OS maps are listed for each walk and as well as helping you find your way these fascinating documents can tell you much about the area in which the walk is set. As a matter of course, carrying a map and compass, and the knowledge of how to use them, will help prevent getting mislaid (never lost) while good walking boots or stout shoes are highly recommended for all walking. Walkers who normally use miles should note that a metre is about 1.1 yards and a kilometre about 0.6 miles.

I strongly advise that at any time of year walkers carry a full set of waterproofs, some extra food and warm clothing, a small First Aid kit and a survival bag as a minimum in case of emergency. Many of the walks follow paths close to natural and man-made hazards, cliff edges and river banks, farm works, quarries etc, where appropriate care is necessary, especially if you have children with you, if accidents are to be avoided.

Rights and Responsibilities

I have done my best to ensure all the walks are on public paths and rights of way or, where this is not the case, that the landowner's permission has been granted. Please try to keep to the route described and follow the Country Code at all times.

It should be noted that, at times, the route described may not exactly follow the paths shown on the excellent Ordnance Survey maps. This can be explained by various factors including "common usage" and locally agreed diversions, permissive paths and, in open country, agreed access. Errors on the maps are rare. Occasionally, paths will change and if a new diversion is in place the route may be diverted from that shown on the map or described in the text.

Remember that some paths will have other user rights – on bridleways you can expect to meet horses and cyclists as well as other walkers, while you may also meet vehicles on some of the "green lanes".

Should you have any problem in following any of the routes due to unreasonable diversion or obstruction of a right of way, send full details (including grid references) to the Welsh Officer of the Ramblers' Association, Ty'r Cerddwyr, High Street, Gresford, Wrexham, LL12 8PT; Telephone 01978 855 148.

Looking after the Countryside

Treat it as a privilege to be able to walk across someone else's land and an atmosphere of co-operation, not confrontation, can be forged. Please:

- Avoid disturbing wildlife
- Do not pick flowers
- Take your rubbish – and any you find – home with you
- Take only photographs – leave only footprints

The Country Code

- Guard against all risk of fire
- Fasten all gates
- Keep dogs under proper control
- Avoid damaging fences, hedges and walls
- Keep to paths across farmland
- Leave no litter
- Safeguard water supplies
- Protect water supplies
- Protect wildlife, wild plants and trees
- Go carefully on country roads
- Respect the life of the countryside

Seals – a special note

As several of the walks in this book are along the Pembrokeshire coast, please note the following extract from The Dyfed Wildlife Trust's "The Grey Seal Code of Conduct".

If you come across a seal on the beach:

- Withdraw immediately and leave it alone.
- Do not fuss around the pup – the mother will probably be watching anxiously from the safety of the waves, and may abandon the pup if humans are in the vicinity.
- Do not let other people disturb the pup.
- Keep dogs well away.
- Do not move or handle the pup, drive it off the beach, try to get it into the sea, feed it, or try to take it home (seals can give a very nasty bite).

If you think the pup has been abandoned:

- Retire and observe from a distance (preferably down-wind) to see if the mother returns, and keep others from disturbing the pup. If the mother does not return within 4 hours, call the RSPCA/Dyfed Wildlife Trust Seal Network (number below).

If the pup is obviously sick or injured:

- Call the RSPCA/Dyfed Wildlife Trust Seal Network immediately on 01990 555 999, do not try to move it or care for it yourself. If you find a dead seal, do not handle it as it may carry infectious diseases. Call the Strandings Line immediately on 01348 875 000

1: Poppit and Ceibwr Circular

Distance: 12½ miles (19.5km)

Time: 6-7 hours

Maps: OS Landranger 145 Cardigan and surrounding area; OS Pathfinder 1010 Cardigan and Dinas Island; OS Outdoor Leisure 35 North Pembrokeshire

Start: Poppit Sands Car Park 152485

Terrain: Cliff path, green lanes, dunes; occasionally very muddy in places.

Nearest town: Cardigan

Parking: See Start

Refreshments: Poppit car park café in season. Webley public house, Poppit.

Suitable for: Older children; dogs on leads.

Along the way

The walk takes in a variety of scenery from the high and convoluted cliffs of the Pembrokeshire Coast Path, quiet lanes and tracks, and the sand dunes of Poppit. There is a certain amount of walking on tarmac at the start of the walk, but this quiet lane from Poppit, for much of its length having grass down the centre, is as much used by walkers as by vehicles.

The inland part of the day's walk is much flatter and easier going than the Coast Path with none of the roller coaster effect, and on old maps most of the green lanes are marked as road. In dry weather the surfaces are good, but in winter the parts used by tractors tend to have a layer of "yeuch" boot-deep on top of the hard surface. Gaiters are highly recommended.

The character of the walk changes dramatically as you leave the coast behind and once the cliffs are out of sight, you are in rolling

Pembrokeshire Coastal Path, Cemaes Head

farmland laced with hedges containing a marvellously diverse and colourful selection of wild flowers.

The Walk

1. Starting in Poppit by the plaque commemorating the opening of the Pembrokeshire Coast Path (which actually starts about 1½ miles further back towards St Dogmaels), the first 1¼ miles of the day's walk is on a narrow metaled road that climbs, at first steeply, up past the Youth Hostel, becoming rougher the further you go until you leave it at the farm campsite at Allt y Goed.

2. From there you climb out onto the headland of green fields, bracken, gorse and wild flowers. Although the views have been good from the lane, the view from Cemaes Head is superlative, looking down on the Teifi Estuary, Cardigan Island and Mwnt to the north-east, and across to Strumble Head in the south-west.

   The Coast Path is mainly in excellent condition, and if you have a head for heights you can look down on boulder-strewn coves

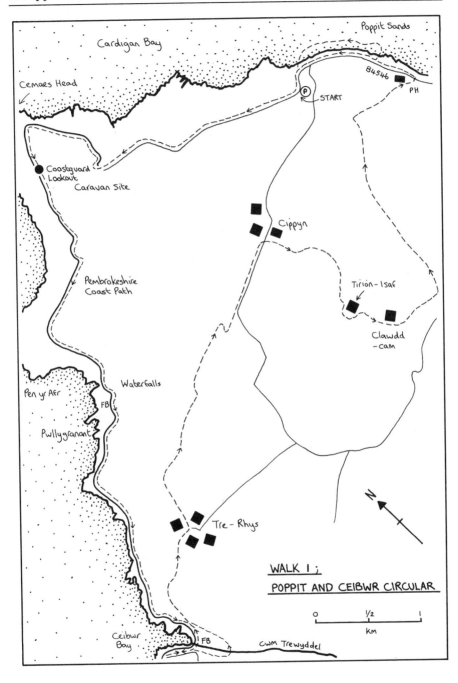

Poppit Sands

Cardigan Bay

Cemaes Head

B4546

PH

P
START

Coastguard
Lookout
Caravan Site

Cippyn

Tirion-Isaf

Clawdd
-cam

Pembrokeshire
Coast Path

Waterfalls

Pen yr Afr

FB

Pwllygranant

Tre-Rhys

N

Ceibwr
Bay

FB

Cwm Trewyddel

WALK 1 ;

POPPIT AND CEIBWR CIRCULAR

0   ½   1
Km

famous for their seal nurseries, while birds such as choughs, herring gulls, greater black-backed gulls, jackdaws, ravens, kestrels, buzzards and, if you are lucky, the odd peregrine, command the air. Much evidence of badger and rabbit diggings are observed along the Coast Path and several examples are seen between here and Ceibwr.

This is one of the more demanding sections of the Coast Path and as you make your way to Ceibwr the ground climbs and dips dramatically, while the cliffs display a text-book example of rock folding of their 400,000,000 year-old Caledonian geology.

3. In the summer of 1993 severe storms caused flash floods that washed away several sections of the path, notably at Pwll y Grannant, and a great deal of work both here and at other shorter stretches of storm damage, has been needed to realign and repair washed-out sections.

   Stone walls, generations old, were swept away in the floods and normally trickling streams gouged four foot deep channels, while earth slips carried large sections of path towards the sea. New bridges, stiles and, in places, board-walk have been built and the path re-cut. Originally a mini bulldozer carved the majority of the path, giving the excellent level surface, but the new work appears to have mainly been created manually.

4. At Pen Castell, from where an Iron Age fort once dominated the bay, obvious cliff falls have severely reduced the amount of fort remaining and the descent to Ceibwr is now different to what is shown in some guides. You have the choice of a steep, often muddy, zigzag to the beach, or a slightly longer, easier track inland to cross the stream by a metaled track at Gaer Wen. If the tide is in and the bridge at the beach not repaired, this latter is the best choice as the stepping stones in place flood out.

5. The south-west side of Ceibwr (N.T.) provides a flat grassy area ideal for an early lunch stop and a view up the coast with a marvellous vista of twisted cliff formations. In rough weather the crashing waves are spectacular.

   The next section of the route climbs back up the Coast Path to

Pen-Castell, but instead of regaining the cliff path, follows the rough track to Tre-Rhys Farm.

6. There is a short length of metaled road, but turning for Hendre at the farm you find yourself on a green (often more a brown "chocolate mousse" after rain) lane heavily used by tractors. This improves as you near the charming duck pond at Hendre.

7. From Hendre to Grannant-Isaf the field track is almost invisible as you cross a field of horses and have a slightly awkward stream/fence crossing below some washed-out reservoirs. Managing this dry shod is not too difficult, though a stile and bridge would be welcome. Once you find your way through or round the collection of farm buildings, ancient and modern, comprising Grannant-Isaf, you are back on a green lane. Some ingenuity may be needed to negotiate this at the obvious dog-leg where it is rather obstructed, though the old dog fox I saw here had no problems.

8. After this green lane a road is followed to just past the chapel at Cippyn. Here you cross into a large field, keeping to the right-hand hedge line, until you enter yet another green lane. Lined with ancient oak trees, this lane leads towards Pantirion Farm and provides a pleasant spot for a late lunch. The lane is left just before you get to the farm and you descend to the stream – more erosion from the storm evident here – and climb past badger setts in a rather neglected blackthorn hedged path to Tirion Isaf from where a well-surfaced track leads past Clawdd-Cam to a crossroads of tracks and green lanes.

9. The route here goes left into yet another green lane, this time quite badly overgrown but still passable. For the first three-quarters of a mile or so this can be very wet after rain, but improves greatly to lead past Manian Fawr to the road above the Webley Hotel. If you are not too muddy at this stage, I recommend the bar here for a refreshment stop before the final stretch back to the car park and café at the start.

10. If the tide is full in you are best off following the road as the track and ford onto the beach floods and crossing can be difficult, but

if the tide is out, the dunes or beach itself offer excellent walking. The ford was washed out in the storms, but the stream is fairly easy to cross a little upstream at low tide and an obvious path leads the way to where a beam may or may not be usable as a bridge, depending on the stream level.

Poppit Sands is popular in and out of season, and as you walk back to the start, you will probably meet more people than in the rest of the day's walking.

2: A Walk around Cilgerran

Distance: 6½ miles (11km)

Time: 3-4 hours

Maps: OS Landranger 145 Cardigan and surrounding area; OS Pathfinder 1010 Cardigan and Dinas Island and 1011Newcastle Emlyn and Llechryd

Start: OS 197429 – Coracle Centre Car Park. Follow signs "to the river" from main village street.

Terrain: Mixed riverside, rural and woodland. Muddy in places, cut branches on path on short sections of the woods make walking a bit awkward.

Nearest town: Cardigan

Parking: See Start

Refreshments: Cafés and pubs in Cilgerran

Stiles: 22, most easy, though some difficult, especially for dogs.

Suitable for: Children and most walkers. No dogs allowed in churchyard.

Along the way

Cilgerran Castle is a neat ruin dating from around 1223 and now in the care of "CADW". A previous castle on this site was the scene of the abduction of Nest (the Welsh "Helen") from her Norman husband by a Welsh prince. Standing high on a crag over the River Teifi, the castle gives terrific views and is worth a visit. Tel 01239 615136. Key to gate available from nearby shop.

In the grounds of the charming Cilgerran Church there is an ancient stone – with inscription still visible – set amongst more modern gravestones on the south side of the church.

Look out for buzzards, signs of badgers and wonderful flowers and fruits along the way.

The Walk

1. After studying the information boards at the Coracle Centre, take the lower path signposted "riverside walk" (note use of bilingual signs and information panels) until you come to a stream that joins the river. Take the steps up to a railed platform with another information board, then from the top of the steps a steep path climbs up under the castle walls, then around the castle to the main gates.

Ancient grave stone, Cilgerran church

2. Turn left here, then first right and stroll down the quiet road for 350 metres to the 13th century church of St Llawddog. Take the main path around the church and leave by a gate in the S.W. corner of the churchyard. A well-maintained path takes you to another gate and onto the road.

   Turn left, then after 25 metres cross over and take the track between a white cottage and a stone barn with blocked-up windows.

3. Follow this track to just short of Penrallt Fach Farm where the path has been diverted over a fence and into a field. Go diagonally down across the field, through a gate in the corner, then follow the left-hand hedge to a well way-marked gate in the far top corner.

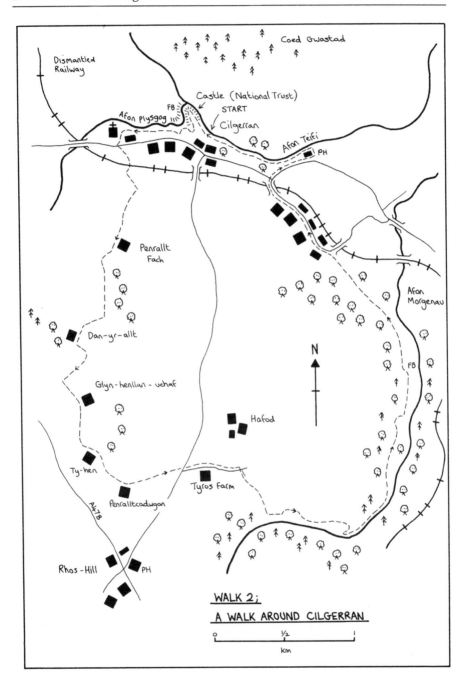

Coed Gwastad

Dismantled
Railway

Castle (National Trust)
START
Cilgerran

FB
Afon Plysgog

Afon Teifi

PH

Penrallt
Fach

Afon
Morgenau

Dan-yr-allt

FB

N

Glyn-henllan - uchaf

Hafod

Ty-hen

Tyros Farm

A478
Penralltcadwgan

Rhos-Hill

PH

WALK 2;
A WALK AROUND CILGERRAN

0   ½   1
km

Turn right after going through the gate, onto a path between high hedges down to a stream. Splash across, then turn left and go through a gateway into a field. Follow the left-hand hedge to a gap in the far hedge line to the next field.

Cross this field to a gate and stile, then across the next field to an obvious gap in the hedge. Keeping on the same line across the next field brings you to a stile and gate made from a pallet. Once over this stile skirt two ponds on a raised embankment, then follow the right-hand hedge to a gate onto a track. Follow the track to a stile 10 metres past a gate on your left where the track curves right.

Take the stile into the field on your left and climb up right to a stile onto the farm track by Dan Yr Allt Farm.

4. Follow the track uphill and along for 300 metres to a staggered cross-roads of tracks. Go left then through the first gate on your right into a field.

Follow the left-hand hedge up to the corner. Do *not* go through the gateway, but cross a stone step stile to its right.

Again follow the left-hand hedge until you come to the far corner. Do *not* go through the metal gate into the lane, but take the stone step stile or gate to your left.

Follow the right-hand hedge for 50 metres, then cross a gate and stile to join an obvious path that swings in a loop around the farm of Ty Hen to join a wide track under some mature trees.

5. Turn left on the track and left again at the stream. Cross the stream on the plank bridge and climb up the bank to a stile.

Turn left and take the path to a stile into the next field, Turn right and follow the hedge and fence to a gate by the barn that brings you into a barn yard. Turn left and take the gate onto a good track which leads to a road.

Turn left, then right down a road signposted "Rhosygilwen", take the first right signposted "Rhosygilwen Farm", then when the main track turns left 150 metres further on, keep straight on and into Rhosygilwen Woods.

6. Follow the track as it bears left, but where it turns down to the right, turn left, then immediately right on a smaller track under a stone wall at the top of the slope.

   Follow this path for about 500 metres when you find it zigzags down the slope to the unusual landmark of an abandoned JCB digger.

7. Turn left here and follow the track through the trees. After a little more than half a mile you come to an iron gate where the path is diverted left around a house, swinging back to rejoin the track across fields on the far side.

   Follow the track past a second house, then where the track goes through a gate and turns right, take the stile on the left before the gate and climb up to join the track that runs northwards behind a ruined cottage.

   This new path winds through attractive broad leaf woodland, but past a ruined mill it becomes a little faint. If you have difficulty, keep headed north-west-ish and do not cross any boundary banks or fences, and you will come, via a footbridge and flight of steps, to the road at Llwyncelyn, 700 metres beyond the mill.

   Turn left on joining the road and follow it for 600 metres into the village. At the T-junction by "Dog Food Dan's" turn right, then 150 metres further on turn left down the side of the "Masons Arms" public house.

8. The track you are on is an old slate extraction ramp from the quarries below that had their heyday in the 19th century.

   On reaching the riverside path at the bottom of the ramp, turn left and you will reach the start of the walk after approximately 700 metres.

3: Bwlchygroes and Ffynone

Distance: 5 miles (8km)

Time: 2½ hours

Maps: Landranger 145 Cardigan and surrounding area; Pathfinder 1034 Boncath, Capel Iwan and Rhos

Start: Bwlchygroes cross-roads SN 240360

Terrain: Field paths, forestry tracks, mainly gentle slopes, can be muddy

Nearest town: Cardigan

Parking: Ample roadside parking on grass verge

Refreshments: Village shop only

Stiles: 6, mostly poor

Suitable for: All, especially children. Dogs on leads. Tree bridge over stream may be difficult for the far-from-agile.

Along the way

Ffynone Waterfall, just over half-way round this short walk, makes an excellent spot for a picnic. Here the Afon Dulas crashes through a narrow gorge of rock and wooded slopes into a pleasant pool where a gravel spit, shade trees, rock and a ruin combine to make an enchanted spot.

The fallen, but live, oak tree that makes a bridge, plus the safe paddling and exploration of the rocks will keep children amused for hours. Although quite well-known locally, Ffynone Waterfall is normally very peaceful and quiet, an excellent lunch stop.

Ffynone Lake was formed as an ornament to the valley by damming the Afon Dulas, during the days of the large estates, and powered a pump house lower down the valley as well as making a

Ffynone waterfall

fish pool and flight pond for various wildfowl. The lake is now silting up but is still attractive and a home for wildlife.

The area around the waterfall is occasionally used by members of the "Alternative Culture" for various ceremonies.

The Walk

1. From the crossroads, take the road headed south for 150 metres to just before the village name sign. Turn right through the right of two gates and head south-westwards keeping to the left-hand hedge to a gate in the corner of the field. Go through this and straight across the next field to a gateway at the end of the hedge marked by a holly tree.

   Go along the grassy track that becomes an un-surfaced and tree lined lane and follow this to Dyffryn Cefn Faes Farm, through the farmyard onto the farm drive and eventually to the road.

2. Turn right here and go up to the crossroads. Cross directly over, not down the opposite road but to behind the signpost where a

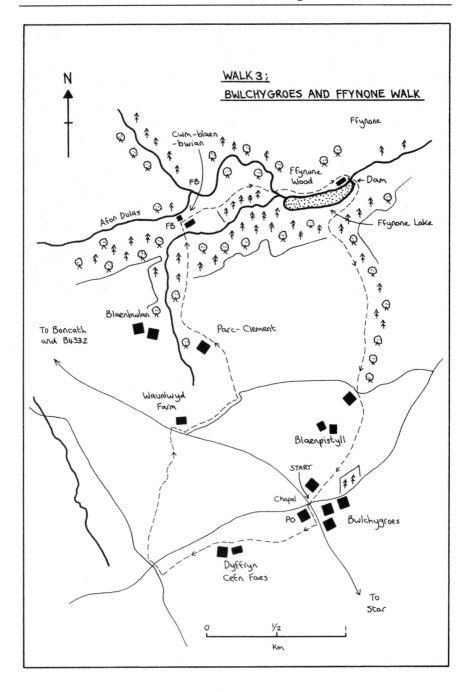

N

WALK 3;
BWLCHYGROES AND FFYNONE WALK

Ffynone

Cwm-blaen
-bwian

FB

Ffynone
Wood

Dam

Afon Dulas

FB

Ffynone Lake

Blaenbwlan

Parc-Clement

To Boncath
and B4332

Waunlwyd
Farm

Blaenpistyll

START

Chapel

PO

Bwlchygroes

Dyffryn
Cefn Faes

To
Star

0   ½   1
              Km

green track between a ruin and field (often with a collection of boats visible) goes up to a field.

Cross into the lane – there is no stile but access is easy if you first go into the field on the right as the intervening hedge is full of wide gaps – to follow it northwards, keeping to the right-hand hedge line when you enter the field. At the far corner this becomes a track again where you cross into the next field. Unfortunately, neglect has allowed this sunken and hedged green lane to become overgrown in many places, and the path now keeps to its eastern side as it zigzags down northwards to the road by Waunlwyd Farm.

3. At the road turn right, then after 100 metres turn left down a quiet lane. Follow this lane as far as a double bend. After the first left-hand bend do not go right along the road, but straight on down a dirt track to Parc Clement Farm. In the valley to the left there are the remains of a mediaeval chapel.

4. Follow the track past the farm and through a gate, and bear right into a field. The left-hand hedge is in fact an overgrown and often flooded green lane, though the path is way-marked in a north-north-westerly direction to a gap in the hedge. Cross into the next field (again the left-hand hedge is the overgrown lane) and after about 125 metres, a gate by a ruin allows you access into the green lane where the Economic Forestry Group land starts. Note the sign by the gate!

5. This well-used path is now followed northwards crossing a forestry road through a dilapidated gate and over a small stream to Cwm-Blaen Bwlan.

Here the main path turns right across the front of the buildings, but, a little further on, where the most-used track turns sharp left, carry straight on up a grassy hedged track that runs alongside a barn.

6. After crossing an iron gate the path keeps to the top of a bank above a forestry plantation for 250 metres, before crossing a poor stile and dropping down to an even more awkward one into the plantation by a faint path alongside the right-hand fence.

7. In the forest. the path is faint but followable, orange/pink paint daubs on the trees helping lead you down to Ffynone Waterfall. The ruins and traces of a structure by the rocks suggest there was once a mill here. Cross the stream either by splashing across, or by the tree bridge to gain a good track running above the stream and lake past old kennels to a cottage and track junction.

   Turn right here, then follow the track as it skirts the lake and then gently climbs south-west. After about 400 metres on this track you come to a T-junction of tracks. Turn left and climb gently up through mixed woodland for three-quarters of a mile up to the road.

8. Turn left, then immediately right up a track, almost opposite the track you came up, past a large white house. This leads up past Blaen Pistyll Farm, back to Bwlchygroes and your car.

   Keep an eye out for buzzards, badgers, foxes, sparrowhawks, goldcrests and wild flowers. This part of Wales is rich in flora and fauna.

4: Around Frenni Fawr

Distance: 6 miles (9.5km)

Time: 3 hours

Maps: OS Landranger 145 Cardigan and surrounding area; OS Pathfinder 1033 Newport (Trefdraeth) and Eglwyswrw and 1034 Boncath, Cape Iwan and Rhos

Start: Roadside layby by "Blaen Nos", grid ref 189 359

Terrain: Mainly good paths. Can be very muddy in places. One optional steep ascent and descent.

Nearest town: Cardigan

Parking: See Start

Refreshments: Castellan Farm "Antiques Teas"

Stiles: 17, many avoidable, all in good condition

Suitable for: All. Dogs on leads.

Along the way

Frenni Fawr dominates the landscape in all directions, so it is not surprising that there are Bronze Age tumuli on the summit. Although these were excavated, no corroboration of the legend of a lead chest filled with gold – supposedly guarded by a storm-bringing phantom – was reported. However, the "Tywyth Teg" or fairies who have been encountered by the burial mounds may of course have moved it. In the past Frenni Fawr with its superb views has been used as a beacon point.

This walk is on mainly good paths, though it can be very muddy in places after rain, and is well way-marked with good views. Look out for the stile that no longer has a fence. Wildlife includes buzzards, foxes, butterflies, goldcrests and various insects. Look out for mushrooms in the season.

The way to the top: Frenni Fawr

The Walk

1. From the lay-by leave the main road by the minor road headed south-east following the signs for Antiques and Teas. Take the first left again heading north-east along a delightful lane with species-rich hedgerows, past Castellan Farm – home of teas, antiques and horses – to the road-end at the stream.

2. From here continue up the track ahead to Dol-Newydd Farm. Cross the yard, keeping to the far side from the house, and enter a sometimes muddy field. Follow the left-hand (northern) hedge for about 150 metres to the corner then cross the stile and bridge into the next field to the north.

   Follow the left-hand hedge of this field northward for 250 metres into a small copse of trees, then on reaching the corner, turn right and go almost due east for 700 metres on intermittently obvious paths crossing three boundaries by difficult stiles or easily climbed/opened gates.

3. This leads out of open fields onto a "green" lane by Cilgoed-Fach. Continue eastwards for 300 metres along the lane, then at the T-junction of lanes turn right (south) and start the easy climb up to a stile/gate 500 metres away at the end of the lane.

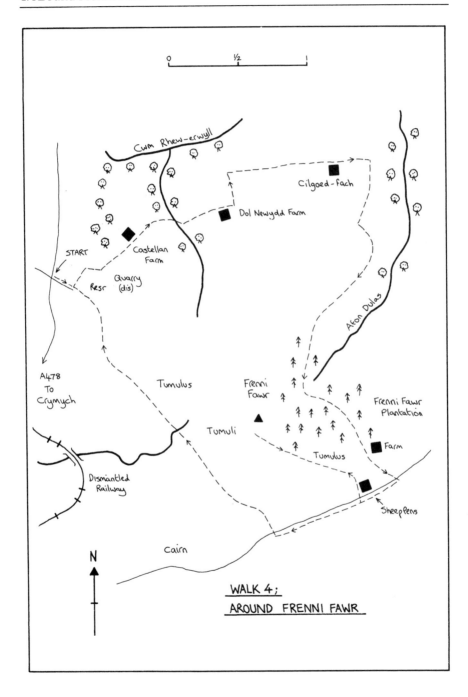

WALK 4;
AROUND FRENNI FAWR

4. Turn left (south-east) into the field and head for the next stile. From here bear right, slightly uphill, and you will soon find yourself on a well-graded if, in places, muddy path that winds along south-westward above the valley and into Frenni Fawr plantation 800 metres further on. This track was once a well-used road, but is now only really passable on foot, having never been surfaced.

5. Once in the plantation follow the main track that swings south, then south-east. Do not drop left but keep to the upper path until it brings you out 900 metres later at a cleared area that is nearly all bulldozed tracks. Head south-east from here, not following the obvious farm/forestry track, but the right of way over the hedge in the field on your right (south-west). This takes you onto the road. Turn right (south-west-ish) and then after 300 metres cross into the field on the right, opposite the road junction, and follow the way-marked route up to the summit of Frenni Fawr.

6. This stiff half mile climb and half mile descent back to the point where you leave the road, give superb views but they can be left out (along with the views) by those too tired or pressed for time. If a group has one member not keen on the climb, they can guard the climbers' rucksacks!

   Back on the road continue south-westward for about 600 metres to a gate onto a well-made track, opposite a road junction. Take this way-marked track north and follow the route – again a deserted road – as it swings around the west side of Frenni Fawr, leaves fields behind and enters onto open hillside.

7. The trees you see on the south-west side of the hill are oak, stunted and dwarfed by their position. As the path heads north-west keep to the obvious way-marked route that keeps close to the boundary between improved pasture and open hill grazing, though in places mud may force diversions.

8. Leaving the hill, the path starts descending and enters a green lane between fields. This drops down to the tarmac road about 200 metres from your vehicle by the turn to Castellan Farm.

   Your choice now – car or cream tea?

5: Nevern

Distance: 3 miles (5km)

Time: 4 hours

Maps: OS Landranger Sheet 145 Cardigan and Surrounding Area; OS Pathfinder 1033 Newport (Trefdraeth) and Eglwyswrw; OS Pathfinder 1010 Cardigan (Aberteifi) and Dinas Head; OS Outdoor Leisure 35 North Pembrokeshire

Start: Nevern Church 083400

Terrain: Good paths and tracks, in fields, muddy in places

Nearest town: Cardigan and Newport

Parking: Limited on roadside at start. Large car park at the Trewern Arms for customers.

Refreshments: Trewern Arms

Stiles: 5

Suitable for: All. Dogs on leads and children under control on river bank

Along the way

Nevern is a small, quiet village in Pembrokeshire and seems very unremarkable until you look more closely. An ancient site of Celtic importance, Nevern loomed out of Celtic mists when "founded" sometime around 1094 by Martin of Tours. This Norman lord built a motte and bailey castle on the site of an Iron Age hill fort above the present village. However, Nevern failed to thrive like Newport down the coast where Martin of Tours founded a second castle after being ousted from Nevern by the Welsh!

Before this time Nevern saw occupation not only by native Celts but also Romans, or Celts of Roman influence, of whom few remains exist. Raids by Vikings who plundered the West Wales coast, saw the old hill fort re-used as a local defence, by the descendants of the Iron Age builders.

In 500-600AD Nevern church was founded by St Brynach, a friend of St David and who communed with angels on top of Carn Ingli, the summit that raises its head above Newport further down river.

Arthurian legends abound in this area and in these tales Meyrick and Cuhelyn are said to have held the stronghold of Nevern while many Welsh folk tales are based on the region. At one time Nevern Castle was held by Rhys Ap Gruffydd, the most powerful prince in South Wales and Henry II's "right loving friend".

When Richard the Lionheart ascended to the throne, Rhys and his unruly sons went on the rampage, over-running many of the South Wales castles. Eventually family quarrels had Rhys imprisoned in Nevern Castle by two of his own sons, but he was released to continue his war against the English, burning towns from Carmarthen to Radnor. On his death in 1197 Rhys was buried in St David's Cathedral. Two years earlier the Castle at Nevern had been destroyed to stop it falling into enemy hands.

The walk itself starts from just outside the church of St Brynach below the castle, and this church itself has many curious and interesting features. Just outside the gates is a mounting block, one of two left in Pembrokeshire, used in the old Welsh wedding custom of the new wife mounting a horse and riding off "pursued" by guests. Were all Welsh wives unwilling?

Passing through the gates of the churchyard you find yourself in the shade of an avenue of English Yews that are contorted by age. The second on the right is the famous "bleeding" yew that weeps copious amounts of red sticky "blood" at certain times of the year. This notable oddity has never been properly explained and is quite a local tourist attraction, as is the great Celtic Cross found nearer the church, on the right.

This cross, probably erected about 1,000 AD stands 13ft tall and is one of the most perfect of its kind. With ribbon decoration in compartments on all four sides, this cross is an excellent example of Celtic art, though on the east side of the cross the mason has made an error in the regularity of the pattern where the "flow" of the ribbon crosses in the main compartment is clockwise on the left-hand arm of the upper cross and all the others are anti clockwise. The two inscriptions come out as "dns" (Dominus – "Lord") and the other perhaps a version of "Hallelujah".

In the outside walls of the church are some interesting stones. On the north wall there is one bearing a partial Latin inscription, probably dating from the latter days of the Roman occupation, while on the east of the porch there is a "bilingual" stone, in both Celtic Ogham script and Latin, called the Vitalianus stone which may date from the 5th century and be one of the oldest of these stones existing. The inscription reads, in Latin "Vitaliani Emereto" in Ogham "Vitaliani" and means (the monument) of Vitalianus. "Emereto" may be an ungrammatical and corrupt version of "discharged with honour".

The charming church, which was founded in 500-600 AD is now mainly Norman but contains work of many periods. Inside there are two more famous stones, found in the sills of the windows in the South transeptal chapel, which itself has an unusual stone vaulted ceiling. One is an unusual form of Celtic cross with a branching and reuniting ribbon pattern, and is 15.5cm x 30.5cm with a triangular head and arms. The other is the "Maglocunus Stone" which, discovered in the fabric of the church in 1906, was one of the bilingual stones that acted as the key to translating Ogham script. The inscriptions, both in Latin and Ogham, translate as "(the monument) of Maglocunus (Maelgwyn) son of Clutorius" but are difficult to make out in poor light. Again this is probably a 5th century AD stone, of great historical importance.

The church and grounds have many more interesting features and time spent here, with the guide available in the church, will give a fuller appreciation of this curious spot.

The Pilgrims' Cross, which is easy to miss, is cut in relief into the rock outcrop 35 metres from the road and was probably a wayside shrine on the Pilgrims' Route from Holywell to St David's, at one time an important pilgrimage destination, and is now almost unique. A little way past the cross are traces of footprints worn into the path by countless feet choosing the same footholds on a rocky section.

The Pilgrim's Cross

One step has a cross cut into it. Nearby there is said to be a walled-up cave containing part of the cross of Christ's crucifixion.

These days the castle is overgrown with ash, oak, beech and other trees and with a wide variety of wild flowers blossoming in the spring. These woods house many bird species from jays to tree creepers, while foxes, badgers and squirrels may also be seen.

Although little stonework remains, the broad layout of the castle, with its moat, walls and towers, as well as an "inner castle" with precipitous slopes to the stream below and a dry ditch giving it extra protection, are still obvious by their mounds. There is a good path exploring the castle and a guide explaining its history is available from the house just below the castle walls.

The Llwyngwair Hotel, which the route passes, was once the family seat of the Bowen family and dates from the 15th century. In the village the bridge and pub the "Trewern Arms" are both worth a brief look (or longer if it is lunchtime!).

The outward route mainly follows the old Pilgrim Route, the return a carriage drive from the Manor to the village. It is rare to find so many significant and curious artifacts along with so much natural beauty in such a small area. This is certainly a short walk ... with much to see in this curious location.

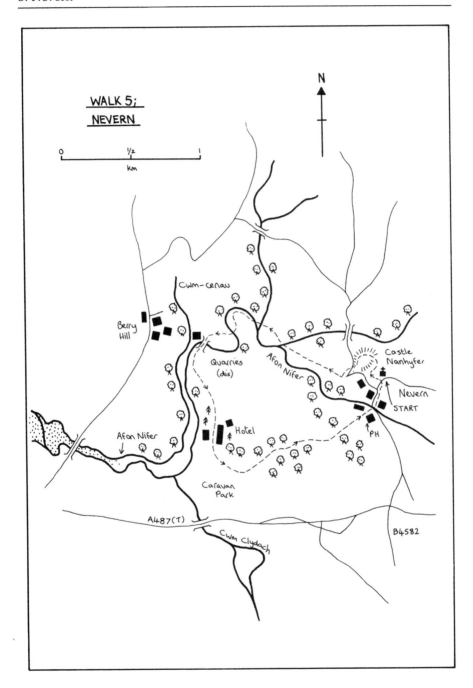

WALK 5;
NEVERN

The Walk

1. Start at the Church. After exploring thoroughly, leave the
   churchyard by the gate behind the tower. Cross the stream by
   the footbridge and take the gravelled track opposite.

   After 50 metres leave this track by the stile on your right and
   follow the way-marked path up to the Castle, which also de-
   serves exploration. Leave the Castle grounds by a gate onto a
   minor road and turn left downhill. Where the road doubles back
   to Nevern, take the path signed "Pilgrims' Cross", joining the
   Pilgrims' Route.

2. Follow this past the cross and steps. The well-marked path leads
   you by fields and riverside paths down to Glandwr where a small
   stream is crossed on a good footbridge.

   From here the path goes along the right-hand side of a cottage
   and continues down along the river side. At times the path floods
   here and an awkward detour up the bank is required.

   On reaching a derelict cottage, the path leaves the river and takes
   a lane along the foot of a slope to the cottages at Pont Newydd.

3. On reaching the wide track here, turn left and follow the track
   over the bridge and down to Llwyngwair Manor.

4. Just past the buildings, take the way-marked path to your left up
   to a gate and stone step stile and onto the old carriage road.

   This leads through woods and to a green lane (take the centre of
   three gates to leave the woods), on through a mass of rhododen-
   drons and across a meadow to come out at a gate and stile at the
   road by Nevern Bridge. Turn left over the bridge to gain the start
   of the walk at the church, or right to visit the Trewern Arms.

6: Cwm Clydach, Tycanol and Carn Ingli

Distance: 8 miles (13km)

Time: 4 to 5 hours

Maps: OS Pathfinder 1033 Newport (Trefdraeth) and Eglwyswrw; OS Landranger 145 Cardigan and Surrounding area; OS Outdoor Leisure 35 North Pembrokeshire

Start: 071 390 Pont Clydach

Terrain: Field paths and rough hill paths. Muddy in places.

Nearest town: Cardigan/Fishguard

Parking: Large lay-by at start

Refreshments: None

Stiles: 12

Suitable for: All. Dogs on leads. Dogs may find the stiles very awkward.

Note: All section of this walk not on Rights of Way are by permission of the Barony of Kemes. Please do nothing to abuse this permission or it may be withdrawn in future. All dogs on leads please.

Along the way

Carn Ingli is a holy mountain where St Brynach went to commune with angels, and shows many remains of prehistoric occupation. Views from here are extensive and the "Cairn of the Angels" (as the name roughly translates) dominates the area.

Tycanol woods and the rock outcrops of Carnedd Meibion Owen form part of a nature reserve that has over 300 species of lichens, one-quarter of the total in Britain, and is a very sensitive area. Please keep strictly to the path and keep dogs on leads in this area.

This walk follows mainly well-defined and well-way-marked

Carn Ingli in winter

paths with some finger posts showing times and distances to other points, while yellow arrows abound. Most stiles are in excellent condition, though the paths, especially in Cwm Clydach, can be very muddy in places.

On Carn Ingli some of the route is steep and rocky, though if necessary the section up to the summit can be by-passed by way of good paths lower down.

The Walk

1. Leave the lay-by by the way-marked steps at the eastern end and climb a stile into the field. The rock in the field is held by some to be a Prehistoric standing stone – by others to be a more modern cattle scratching post! Follow the left-hand hedge on a track to top of field and turn left through a metal gate onto a tree-lined track. Turn left and follow the track past the ruins of a farm, note the unusual "bee-hive" shaped fireplace in the left-hand building, and on through a metal gate.

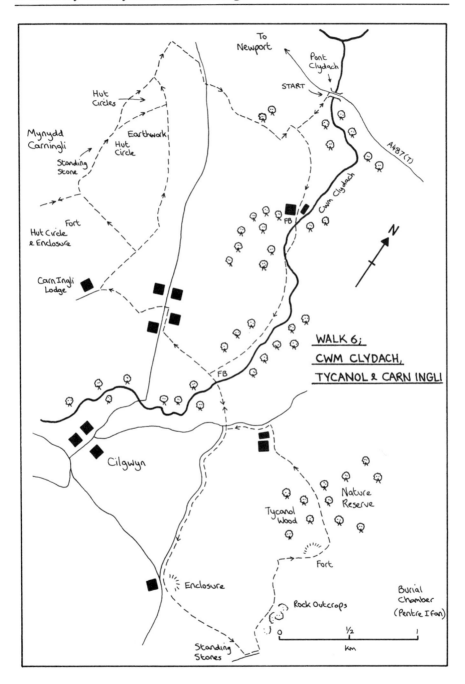

50 metres past this gate you come to a crossroads of paths. Go straight over and descend to Cwm Clydach.

2. At the farm turn left (finger post) and cross the Afon Clydach on a gated footbridge. The path now climbs to the top of the eastern side of the valley, giving excellent views of Carn Ingli before dropping steeply after a wooden gate to re-cross the river on another footbridge.

    The path now zigzags up southwards to a gap in a wall (finger post) and into a field. Follow the bottom edge of the field and enter the woods by a gap in the far wall.

    The path, though indistinct and muddy in places, generally follows the base of the bank in the woods, after 300 metres rising to the top before dipping again to cross some streams, until about 500 metres from entry into the wood you come out into a field again.

    Cross the field, following the way-marks, to a ladder stile into a field full of ruined walls which is crossed to gain an un-surfaced lane by way of an obvious metal gate and ladder stile.

3. Turn left and descend to a ford and footbridge before climbing up to a road junction. Go over the junction, taking the road opposite the lane, climbing south-south-east and giving excellent views. Follow this quiet road for three-quarters of a mile and when you are 10 metres beyond a cottage called Troed-y-Rhiw, a track rises due east by an ancient enclosure and derelict cottages. Follow this track through two gates into an open field and, keeping to the right-hand side of the field, note the standing stones in the field to your right. A "shadow" of this track leads you onto a road by way of a third gate. Turn left, immediately leaving the road for a green lane. 50 metres up this, cross a stile on your left and enter the nature reserve.

4. The obvious rock outcrop is the first of the Carnedd Meibion Owen and the path keeps to the fence that winds up to and behind these rocks.

    Follow the way-marked path north-west behind the rocks, then down to a gate above Tycanol Woods. A near-by "cave" filled with engraved graffiti is said to have been used by St Brynach when he was not on Carn Ingli. Go through the gate and down the side of the woods before entering the woods. 60 metres into the woods go sharp left at the way-mark and follow the fence on your right to a gap in the mossy ruined wall.

5. Take the path way-marked straight on into the heart of Tycanol Wood, crossing the stream gully and following the left rim of the gully.

    After leaving a stone wall, the path bears left and you leave the reserve by two stiles.

    Once in the field head north-west-ish below the ruined wall and cross a stile by a large tree into the next field.

    Leave this field by the gate in the south-western corner (above the farmhouse) and turn right onto a farm track that leads you down to the road.

    Turn left and in 350 metres you will be back at the track/road junction. Turn right, re-cross the river Clydach and follow the lane west to a road.

    Turn right on the road, then after 150 metres turn left up a farm track and through a gate onto a path up the open hillside to another farm road. On reaching this, turn right on a grassy track and after 400 metres you will come to a broad grassy track that climbs left, up to Carn Ingli. To avoid the rocky summit section take the path straight on that skirts the mountain to rejoin the route above Carn Cwn.

    Passing the remains of an old aerial cableway in an area known as "Drum", from the winding gear once used in this short-lived quarrying operation, the path meanders uphill.

6. On reaching the ridge, climb south-west to the summit on rough paths, then after enjoying the views, descend northwards down the ridge and the obvious path towards Newport. This is steep and awkward to start with but improves to a broad grassy ride.

7. A little way short of the gate off the open mountain abandon the main track and drop into the rocks of Carn Cwn. Here, above a

horizontal crack in the main rocks is painted (just visible if you look hard) the legend "wishing well". The well – reputedly tidal! – is inside the crack and is very refreshing, if hard to get at.

Regain the path and go through the gate into a hedged track. After 200 metres turn right onto the lane which leads you to a road. Turn right, then cross over after 100 metres and take the narrow lane descending eastwards.

Follow this lane as it deteriorates. Where the lane divides and becomes un-surfaced go right, then after another 150 metres, abandon it, crossing into the field by a magnificent stile and dropping diagonally down across the field to the woods on a faint path.

In the woods join a broad track and turn east, following the track through the wood. 30 metres after leaving the wood drop north through a gap in the wall (black and yellow way-marks) and keep to the left-hand hedge, descending to another stile.

Cross this into a hedged track, turn right, then after 35 metres turn left through a metal gate and descend the track retracing the start of the walk back to the stile, steps and lay-by.

7: Around Newport

Distance: 10 miles (16km)

Time: 5 to 7 hours

Maps: OS Landranger 145 Cardingan and surrounding area; Pathfinder 1033 Newport (Trefdraeth) and Eglwyswrw; OS Outdoor Leisure 35 North Pembrokeshire

Start: Parrog 051396

Terrain: Coast path and hill tracks. Muddy in places.

Nearest Towns: Fishguard and Cardigan

Parking: Large car parks in both Newport and Parrog.

Refreshments: Cafés and pubs in Newport.

Stiles: Six.

Suitable for: Persons of average fitness. Dogs on leads. Children should be kept under control on cliff sections.

Note: All section of this walk not on Rights of Way are by permission of the Barony of Kemes. Please do nothing to abuse this permission or it may be withdrawn in future. All dogs on leads please.

Along the way

For some truly memorable walks I would suggest you come to Newport in the autumn when the gorse and heather are both in bloom, the weather tends to be good and the mass of grockles have gone home. A breezy day adds an extra touch to the walk, as you will discover, and the rough sea adds excitement.

For those interested in history this walk passes a variety of intriguing sites, including a prehistoric settlement on the banks of the estuary, a cromlech, associated with King Arthur, several pre-

historic cairns, hut circles and enclosures as well as Newport Castle
– now a private residence.

The summit of Carn Ingli, as well as having very obvious remains
of an Iron Age hill fort, is where St Brynach is said to have communed with angels and contains magnetic rocks that can spin a
compass needle.

Looking south-east from Carn Ingl

The Walk

1. The walk starts at Parrog at the bottom end of Newport, before following the side of the river past a prehistoric settlement and turning up past Carreg Coetan Arthur – the cromlech hidden behind some bungalows – and climbing through quiet back lanes, past the castle and church, to gain the open hillside of Carn Ingli by Carn Cwn.

2. If you leave the main track for a moment and go into these rocks, you may find the "wishing well", a narrow horizontal crack in the rocks with an almost inaccessible pool that is reputed to be tidal! At one time the name "wishing well" was painted over the relevant rocks, but this has now faded almost to the point of invisibility.

3. From here regain the obvious grassy track that leads up onto Carn Ingli itself, the haunt of crows and buzzards and where famous Celtic Saint Brynach communed with the angels (hence Carn Ingli – "Angel's Mountain"). This rocky eminence dominates the surrounding countryside and the walls and battlements of the prehistoric fort on this site are still clearly visible.

4. Heading west over the open moor, Carn Briw, the prehistoric cairn on the summit of Carn Ingli Common makes a good viewpoint before the faint paths drop towards Mynydd Caregog, past prehistoric hut circles to Bedd Morris. In snow this is a winter wonderland of strange rock outcrops, and a scattering of snow shows up the hut circles to advantage. However, you cannot beat the colours when both heather and gorse are in full flower.

5. Bedd Morris (Morris' Grave) is a prehistoric site with Iron Age connections, though the standing stone, now a parish boundary and reputedly where Morris, a local sheep rustler was hanged, is probably a much more ancient fertility stone.

    From here the path once again heads west over fields and moorland on a good track past more prehistoric sites, the remains of WWII military emplacements, through some of the worst of

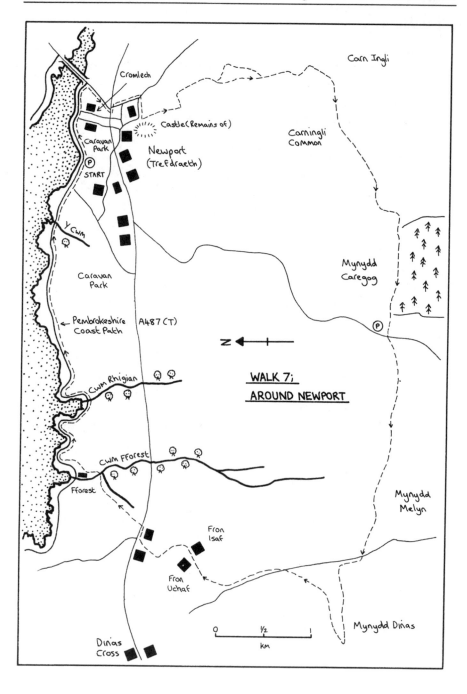

Carn Ingli

Cromlech

Castle (Remains of)

Caravan Park

Newport
(Trefdraeth)

Carningli
Common

START

Y Cwm

Caravan Park

Mynydd Caregog

Pembrokeshire Coast Path

A487 (T)

N

WALK 7;
AROUND NEWPORT

Cwm Rhigian

Cwm Fforest

Fforest

Mynydd Melyn

Fron Isaf

Fron Uchaf

Mynydd Dinas

Dinas Cross

0   ½   1
km

Welsh gates, to climb onto Mynydd Dinas. The route here passes a prehistoric enclosure that is still well-defined.

6. The rocky outcrops of Garn Fawr make an ideal lunch spot with shelter from the wind, extensive views over the Preselis, Fishguard and the coast and the distant hills and islands around St David's. Carved into the rock is a rough cross which, unfortunately, has recently been used as a target for shotgun practice.

7. The walk now starts the homeward stretch, passing the rugged outcrop of Carn Enoch, visible for so long, before dropping down past more well-defined prehistoric enclosures to the minor road to Dinas. The tarmac is soon abandoned by a coastguard radio relay station and the route follows rough farm tracks back down to the A487 past quiet farms where even the geese and dogs are friendly.

   Crossing the road, the route takes the well way-marked footpath opposite the chapel. This leads through a wooded valley to rejoin the coast at Fforest.

8. A windy day is best to experience this section through Cwm Dyffryn, as you pass through an open-air art exhibition "timber, turf and time" where sculptures in natural materials are returning to the ground, and wind chimes ring in the air. Quite magical.

9. After crossing the lip of a weir above a roaring waterfall, the route joins the Coast Path at Fforest.

10. From Fforest, the route follows the Pembrokeshire Coast Path east along the top of the cliffs into steep-sided cwms.

    In the rugged coves below the sheer cliffs you may well see seals and, in the season, the charming seal pups. At other times rough seas make this stretch exhilarating.

8: Cwm Gwaun and Carn Ingli

Distance: 6 miles (5.5km)

Time: Up to 4 hours

Maps: OS Landranger 145 Cardigan and Surrounding Area; OS Pathfinder 1033 Newport (Trefdraeth) and Eglwyswrw; OS Outdoor Leisure 35 North Pembrokeshire

Start: Sychpant car park and picnic site 045349

Terrain: Woodland paths, open hills, muddy in places

Nearest town: Cardigan/Fishguard

Parking: At start

Refreshments: None

Stiles: 12

Suitable for: Persons of average fitness, older children, dogs (on lead at times)

Note: All sections of this walk not on Rights of Way are by permission of the Barony of Kemes. Please do nothing to abuse this permission or it may be withdrawn in future. All dogs on leads please.

Along the way

Carn Ingli is where Celtic St Brynach used to go to pray and commune with angels, the name of the mountain roughly translating as "Cairn of the Angels". An Iron Age fort of great importance, Carn Ingli dominates the area. The summit rocks are magnetic and in places can spin your compass needle – to the detriment of navigation but the amusement of onlookers.

The Gwaun Valley is remote and individualistic. It followed the old Julian Calendar for many years after the Gregorian correction of 1582 was introduced and accepted across Britain.

Looking north-west from Carn Ingli

Sychpant is an important site with rare lichens and plants to be found there. The remains of many habitations are passed on this walk, from prehistoric hut circles to more modern ruined cottages that stand witness to the depopulation of the countryside.

The Walk

This walk starts in the Sychpant picnic site before climbing up through a coniferous wood onto the open hills of Carningli Common and the Iron Age fort of Carn Ingli, before descending again to follow quiet woodland tracks in the beautiful Gwaun Valley. Nowhere too strenuous, this walk takes you through a variety of scenery and past ancient remains. Although many of the paths do not coincide with what is shown on the maps, clear way-marking makes most of this walk easy to follow.

1. Cross over the footbridge between the car park and the toilet block and you come across the first signpost on the walk. Turn right and walk up through the picnic site keeping the stream on your right, picking up further way-marks as you follow an

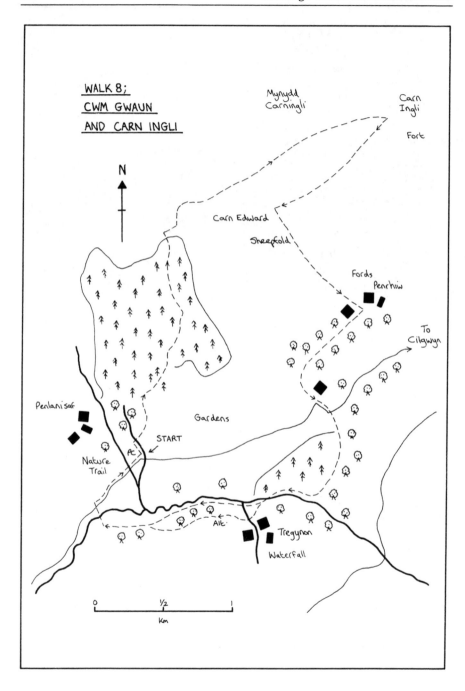

WALK 8;
CWM GWAUN
AND CARN INGLI

N

Mynydd
Carningli

Carn
Ingli

Fort

Carn Edward

Sheepfold

Fords
Penrhiw

To
Cilgwyn

Penlanisaf

Gardens

START

Ac

Nature
Trail

Tregynon

Waterfall

Alt

0   ½   1
       Km

obvious though narrow path that climbs steeply up to the coniferous woodland crossing the stream on the way.

2. Entering the woods over a poor stile, take the clear, if occasionally muddy path, following the sign posts "Carn Ingli" and black way-marks as you climb gently upwards. At the path junction in the middle of the woods, just after a 90 degree bend in the path, leave the black way-marks and follow yellow way-marks and the signpost "Carn Ingli" on the right-hand of the two paths..

    The path is narrow, winding and faint in places, so keep alert so as not to miss any of the way-marks as the path wends its way up through the woods to gain the open hill just east of Mynydd Caregog.

    Crossing the stile in the fence separating hill from woods you keep the fence on your right and head north until you come to a bend in the fence. From here pick your way in a north-easterly direction across heather, gorse and bilberry on narrow trods and across open ground towards the obvious cairn on the summit of Carn Ingli Common called Carn Briw.

3. From Carn Briw, which commands stunning views over Newport Bay, the Gwaun Valley and the Preseli Hills, it is an easy walk over to Carn Ingli fort, the highest point of the day.

4. Turning south-west from Carn Ingli drop down to a track that runs south-west then west above a fence. Follow this until you come to a gate and stile above the outcrop of Carn Edward.

5. Cross the stile and bear left of the rocks until you pick up a grassy track running down to a stile and gate in a wall below. Once you are through the gate a clear path runs down to intersect with an ancient track by Pen Rhiw Farm. Keep the fence on your left and you will find stiles crossing every field boundary on the way.

6. At Pen Rhiw Farm you again come across good way-marking. Follow the sign "Cwm Gwaun 2.0km 45 min" pointing you down along a sometimes muddy lane which comes out at Llanerch Farm in the valley bottom.

    Cross the valley on the road to pick up another way-marked path opposite Llanerch Farm, passing through a muddy gateway to follow a woodland path. This track hugs the bottom of the steep southern valley wall and at all junctions you take the lower option. Very muddy sections have log "duckboards" while a bridge crosses the one major stream.

7. If you wish, you can take a detour on good paths up to Tregynon where there is a prehistoric homestead with interpretation board. After climbing up to the buildings, the path hugs the top of the slope until descending to rejoin the lower path, by now quite faint and narrow, by some ruins.

8. 100 metres past the ruins there is a sign post which points you across a boggy field with the notation "Sychpant CP ½ m". Following this sign you come to a bridge over the Afon Gwaun, and this takes you to two stiles and the valley road. Turn right here and after a quarter of a mile up the road you will be back at your car.

9: Carn Ingli

Distance: 2½ miles (4km)

Time: 3 hours

Maps: OS Landranger 145 Cardigan and surrounding area; OS Pathfinder 1033 Newport (Trefdraeth) and Eglwyswrw; OS Outdoor Leisure 35 North Pembrokeshire

Nearest town: Newport 1½ miles away has pubs, shops and cafés.

Start: Broad, grassy pull-in, map reference 070 373

Terrain: Moorland and a rocky mountain summit. Strenuous.

Parking: See Start.

Suitable for: All

Note: All section of this walk not on Rights of Way are by permission of the Barony of Kemes. Please do nothing to abuse this permission or it may be withdrawn in future. All dogs on leads please.

Along the way

Superb upland walking with tremendous views from an Iron Age fort high point. Carn Ingli is where St Brynach went to commune with angels. Some of the rocks are highly magnetic and one in particular will spin a compass right round.

The "wishing well" is reputedly not only lucky, but also affected by the tides!

Ponies, buzzards and a variety of other birds are always to be seen, while visitors late in the season will see the hills come alive with the bloom of both heather and gorse – a truly beautiful combination.

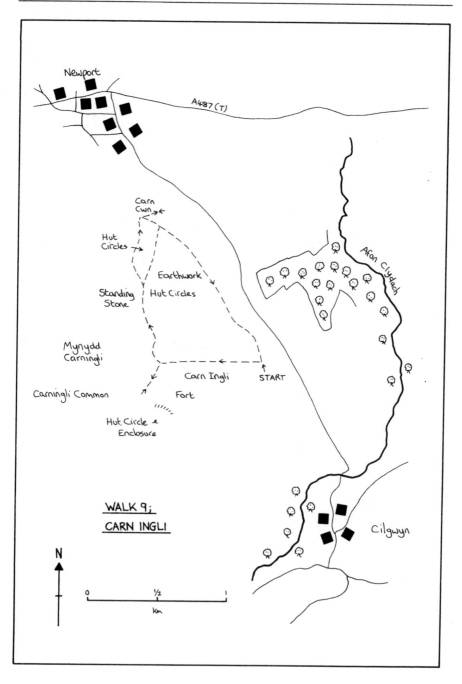

Newport

A487 (T)

Carn
Cwn

Hut
Circles

Earthwork

Standing   Hut Circles
Stone

Mynydd
Carningli

Carningli Common   Carn Ingli   START
                        Fort

Hut Circle &
Enclosure

Afon Clydach

WALK 9;
CARN INGLI

N

0   ½   1
        km

Cilgwyn

The Walk

1. From the pull-in take the obvious grassy path leading straight up the mountain. As this nears the top of the ridge, bear left and pick your way to the very top by a maze of narrow paths through heather and over rocks. You will need to use your hands in places.

2. From the summit retrace your steps and descend the ridge, but bearing left towards the town of Newport below to pick up a clearly visible grassy path. Take care on the steep, narrow, rocky and winding upper part of the path.

3. After crossing a wide path, but before reaching a gate off the open mountain, turn right into the rocks of Carn Cwn. Here you will find a narrow horizontal gap in the main outcrop with "wishing well" (now almost invisible) painted above. The well is in the gap and difficult to get a refreshing drink from.

   Retrace your steps to the wide path already crossed and turn left along it. This runs above the wall, eventually leading you back to the road, some 400 metres short of your car. Turn right and finish the walk on the grassy road edge.

Carn Ingli from the west

10: Dinas Island and Dinas Mountain

Distance: 9 miles (14.5km) or 10 miles (16km) depending on option taken

Time: 5 hours to 7 hours

Maps: OS Land Ranger Sheet 157 St David's and Haverfordwest Area; OS Pathfinder Sheets 1032 Fishguard/Abergwaun, 1033 Newport(Trefdraeth) & Eglwyswrw 1010 Cardigan (Aberteifi) & Dinas Head; OS Outdoor Leisure 35 North Pembrokeshire

Start: Pwllgwaelod 005 398

Terrain: Undulating coast walking, good tracks and paths, muddy in places.

Nearest town: Fishguard

Parking: Pwllgwaelod and Cwm yr Eglwys

Refreshments: None

Stiles: Minimum of 28! Most in very good condition. Most on coast path section. Many by-passable!

Suitable for: Persons of average fitness, older children, dogs on lead for long stretches.

Note: All section of this walk not on Rights of Way are by permission of the Barony of Kemes. Please do nothing to abuse this permission or it may be withdrawn in future. All dogs on leads please.

Along the way

At Cwm yr Eglwys you pass the ruins of St Brynach's, a 12th century Celtic church destroyed in the great storm of 1859 when 113 ships were sunk around Wales. St Brynach is a locally famous saint who communed with angels on Carn Ingli.

In the woods above Fforest there is a sculpture exhibition called "Timber, Turf and Time" by Gareth Walton. The sculptures, in

Cerrig Duon

natural materials, are being allowed to rot back into the environment.

The Walk

This walk starts in the bottom of a glacial meltwater channel that almost cuts Dinas "Island" off from the mainland, follows parts of the Pembrokeshire Coastal Path, climbs through an open air art exhibition onto Dinas Mountain with stupendous views before descending once more to the Coast Path.

1. Right at the car park in Pwllgwaelod you have a choice of paths. You can either take the direct path to Cwm yr Eglwys that runs behind the row of buildings, once "The Sailors' Safety" inn, or take the coast path around Dinas Island (NT) which adds 1½ miles and a stiff climb to the route. Both paths are clearly signposted and the direct route is suitable for wheelchairs.

2. From the ruined church at Cwm yr Eglwys follow the road uphill in front of the house called "Tides Reach" for 400 metres to a

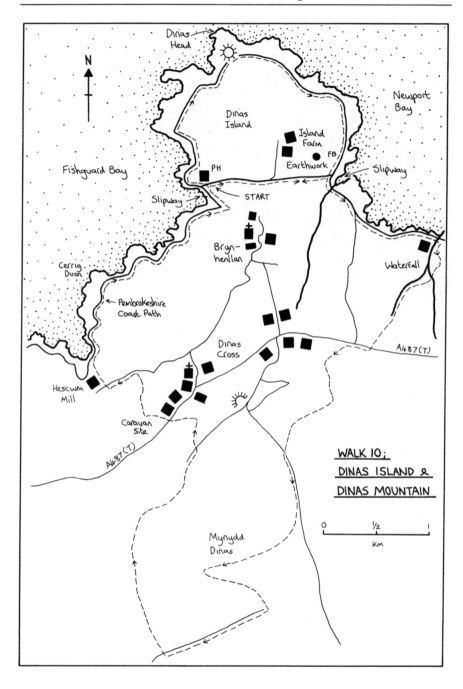

poorly signposted track cutting off eastward by a gate with the name "Perci Penrhiw" in the ironwork. You are now back on the Coast Path which you follow down to the beach in Aber Fforest. Do not follow path up west side of Cwm.

3. Amid confusing and contradictory waymarking, cross the stream by the bridge and enter the field ahead. Leave the Coast Path here and climb to the top right-hand corner of the field, signposted Public Footpath. Exit the field at a track junction and follow the branch marked "house" on a sign-board for about 100 metres before entering the woods just above the sharp turn into the house yard. Follow the wide track into the woods, cross the stream by a concrete dam wall (a weir when in flood) and ignoring the steps ahead, follow the signposted Public Footpath to the right. A diversion to the waterfall is worthwhile.

4. Follow the footpath up through the woods, past ruined cottages and the tumbling structures of an open air art exhibition to the main road. Turn right, then after about 150 metres turn left up a muddy track signposted "Fron Isaf" on the telegraph pole. This track leads you up past and through three sets of dwellings (mind the geese!) before you find yourself on the open hillside.

   300 metres beyond "Fron Uchaf" turn south on a narrower track that crosses in front of a radio relay station to join the road. Turn left (south) and follow the road to the cattle grid.

5. From here you can pick your own route across the open hillside south-west and west via Carn Enoch to Garn Fawr – the highest point on Dinas Mountain – which gives terrific views. Note the cross engraved in the rocks before descending south-east to rejoin the road.

   Follow the road south-west for just over half a mile then turn right up a way-marked footpath through a gate past a house called "Treffynon" and on for 1.8 km. This path crosses above a ruined farm, then contours round the hill heading for the sea. Staying at around the same height as the ruins, the path follows the right hand, uphill, side of the often bouldery wall line, eventually entering a well way-marked narrow green lane, and eventually rejoining tarmac beyond the turn up to Fagwyr Meredith.

6. After about 200 metres of tarmac, climb an iron gate into a field on your left and follow the way-marked path downhill. At the bottom of the bank go through an iron gate and turn left between the buildings, reaching the main road through a small caravan park.

7. Cross the road to pick up a bridle path that zigzags down over a ford to pick up a tarmac lane leading down to Hescwm Mill.

8. Go through the gates and follow the clear path down to the beach at Aber Bach, where, turning right you regain the Pembrokeshire Coast Path that will lead you back to Pwllgwaelod by way of some superb cliff scenery.

11: Llys-y-Fran

Distance: 7½ miles (12km)

Time: 3 hours

Maps: OS Landranger 145 Cardigan and Surrounding Area; OS Pathfinder 1057 Ambleston & Llandissilio; OS Outdoor Leisure 35 North Pembrokeshire

Start: 041 245 (car park)

Terrain: Well-graded path, muddy in places.

Nearest town: Cardigan/Haverfordwest

Parking: See Start

Refreshments: Café/restaurant and gift shop by start, open 9.30 – 5pm in summer (weekends only in winter)

Stiles: None

Suitable for: Children, and dogs on leads. Children's play area by start. Beware of cyclists!

Along the way

The reservoir and country park were opened in 1972 by HRH Princess Margaret and have become a popular attraction. Initially built to serve the Milford Haven oil terminals and refineries, the 187 acre lake is formed by impounding the River Syfynwy behind a 35 metre concrete dam. However, unless you are right beside it, this feature does not intrude on the scene.

The reservoir has a well-graded perimeter track for walking on, replacing a waterside path (as marked on the maps) that became unusable once the water level was raised in the mid '90s. This walk passes through a nature reserve and conservation area with sessile oak woods providing breeding sites for sparrow-hawk, buzzards, woodpeckers, jays and nuthatches, while sitka plantations hold such birds as goldcrests. The reservoir attracts a multitude of water

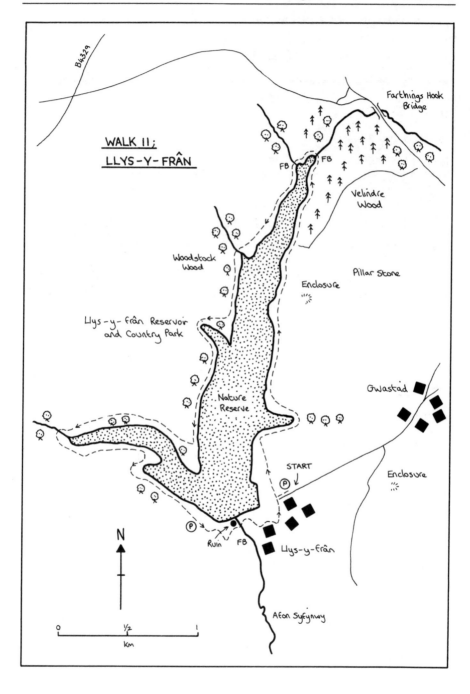

B4329

WALK 11;
LLYS-Y-FRÂN

Farthings Hook
Bridge

FB   FB

Velindre
Wood

Woodstock
Wood

Pillar Stone

Enclosure

Llys-y-frân Reservoir
and Country Park

Nature
Reserve

Gwastad

Enclosure

START

Llys-y-frân

Ruin   FB

Afon Syfynwy

N

0   ½   1
km

Llys-y-Fran reservoir

fowl, while mammals in the area include foxes, badgers, squirrels etc. Insects and wild flowers abound, while sportsmen take part in fishing, bird-watching, canoeing, kayaking, sailing, boardsailing and – occasionally – abseiling off the dam.

Llys-y-Fran translates as "court of crows" and many magpies, crows, jackdaws and rooks can be seen in the area.

The Walk

The walk is very straightforward, following the un-surfaced track that skirts the reservoir. This walk has location and distance markers, picnic benches and information signs scattered along its length, and keeps the walker out of the way of anglers (and vice versa), while giving excellent views of the water and its wildlife. You can descend to the water's edge at many points for a closer look.

1. Starting in the car park the walk turns right opposite the café/shop visitor centre and follows a surfaced track towards the boat park by the play area before cutting off across the open grass on an un-surfaced track.

2. At first quite open, this path is flanked by ancient oak woods as you approach the northern end of the reservoir and, once you cross the footbridge over the river, the character of the walk changes and you find yourself on an undulating and sometimes sinuous path through oak woods with small crags and rocky outcrops.

3. Crossing the smaller streams that join the reservoir, the path can be quite steep as it dips and rises again, while excellent views can be had when the path clears the woodland.

4. The track eventually brings you out at a car park on the west end of the dam and a narrow footpath drops down by the side of the dam to join the road. This winds down past a memorial to William Penfro Rowlands (1860-1937) who was born in the adjacent ruined cottage and wrote the hymn tune Blaenwern, passes the foot of the dam across the now-tamed river and up by the control building (often sporting a huge spout of water) to the café/restaurant and shop, and the start of the walk.

12: Rosebush, Foel Eryr and Foel Cwmcerwyn

Distance: 12½ miles (20km)

Time: 6 hours

Maps: OS Landranger 145 Cardigan and Surrounding Area; OS Pathfinder 1033 Newport (Trefdraeth) and Eglwyswrw; OS Outdoor Leisure 35 North Pembrokeshire

Start: The Old Post Office, Rosebush 075 294

Terrain: Hill tracks, forestry paths. Muddy in places.

Nearest town: Cardigan

Parking: By "Tafarn Sinc Preseli", pub on roadside by start

Refreshments: "Tafarn Sinc Preseli" pub or Old Post Office tea rooms, restaurant and bistro

Stiles: 3

Suitable for: The fairly fit. Dogs on leads

Note: All parts of the route not on Rights of Way, by courtesy of the Barony of Kemes. Please behave responsibly or permission to use these routes may be withdrawn. All dogs on leads please.

Along the way

The small village of Rosebush owes its existence to the now disused quarries that used to provide roofing slate. These have now mellowed into the view and form an interesting site of industrial archaeology.

The old railway was once advertised as a tourist attraction, bringing visitors to admire the wilderness of the Preselis. The "Tafarn Sinc Preseli" is a Victorian hotel built to receive these

Looking east from Foel Eryr

visitors, but no longer offers accommodation in its locally famous corrugated iron walls, now serving only as a pub.

Foel Cwmcerwyn is the highest point in West Wales and has Bronze Age cairns on its summit, while the track along the crest of the Preselis is a prehistoric trade road from Ireland via St David's and Whitesands Bay to Salisbury Plain.

The Walk

1. Leave Rosebush along the track under the old quarries and through a gate into the conifers of the Pantmaenog Forest, turning right on a good forestry track. 250 metres along this track turn left over a small stream and follow the bridleway below the edge of the woods.

2. On rejoining the track 700 metres further on, bear left. Bear left at two further junctions, eventually coming out of the woods onto the open hill and the "Golden Road" at Bwlch Pennant.

3. Go straight on here, following a vague track over boggy terrain.

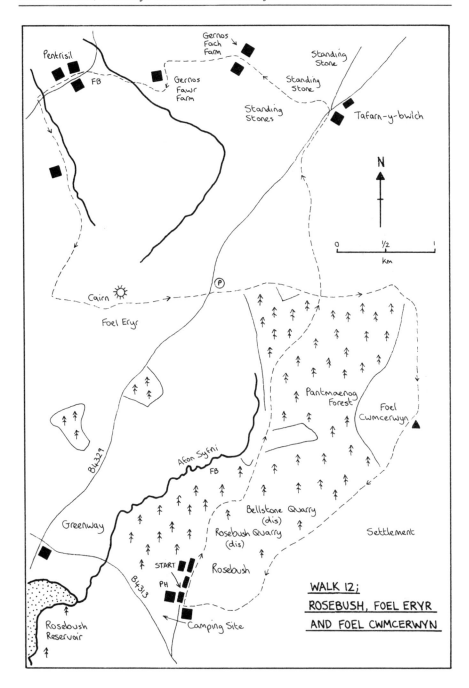

WALK 12;
ROSEBUSH, FOEL ERYR
AND FOEL CWMCERWYN

This is the old road from Tafarn y Bwlch to Rosebush and it becomes a clear track as you descend to the road above the cattle grid at Tafarn y Bwlch.

4. Cross the cattle grid and turn left past the telephone box, through a gate and up a farm track. Note the standing stones on either side of the track At the farm turn left between the buildings and go through a gate into a rough lane. Follow this for about 300 metres before entering fields by a gate.

5. Follow the left-hand hedge, still on an obvious track, for 350 metres then turn left into a sunken green lane that leads you down to Gernos Fawr. Cross the intriguing bridge, go through the farmyard and follow the green track down the valley and past a ruined cottage. Cross the stream at the bottom of the valley by the footbridge, go through a gate and turn left onto a quiet lane.

6. Follow this for 900m, go through a very wet gateway on your left next to the drive to "Buarth Gwyn" and take a rough track across the hillside, keeping the fence on your right. Passing the remains of an old "pit", perhaps a source of road-fill rubble, the path becomes faint until you pass "Pen-lan-wynt" farm where it again becomes obvious. As you walk on, the path gradually fades to faint trods and climbing around the side of Foel Eryr, moves away from the fence across some wet ground. When this track becomes boggy, at the top of a cwm leading north-west, cut up eastward to the summit of the hill by narrow footpaths and faint trods.

7. The summit offers superb views and with its view-finder plaque and Bronze Age cairn is a popular spot for a rest. Follow the wide track eastwards from the summit, dropping down to and crossing the B4329 at "Bwlch Gwynt" and going straight on along the crest of the Preselis, following the Golden Road.

    Keep the forestry on your right as you cross your earlier path and climb on eastwards over rather boggy ground.

8. Keep to the edge of the woods until you reach a stile over a fence running eastwards from the woods. Cross this and take the path that meanders southwards to the summit of Foel Cwmcerwyn.

This is the highest point in West Wales and offers views that can include Snowdonia, the Brecon Beacons, Devon, and even Ireland.

9. From the summit drop southwards to pick up a broad track that follows the forest edge. Keep to this track for 800 metres until a way-marked stile on right. Cross this, and another stile ahead, and bear left onto a good track which takes you down to a farm. Follow the farm track down to Rosebush. Turn right and 50 metres further on you are back at the start of the walk.

13: Preseli Top (Foel Cwmcerwyn) and Rosebush

Distance: 5 miles (8km)

Time: 4 hours

Maps: OS Landranger 145 Cardigan and surrounding area; OS Pathfinder 1033 Newport (Trefdraeth) and Eglwyswrw; OS Outdoor Leisure 35 North Pembrokeshire

Nearest towns: Cardigan and Fishguard

Start: Rosebush, map reference 076 294.

Terrain: Strenuous but rewarding 5 mile walk through forest, moorland and over hills, mainly on good paths.

Parking: Roadside parking by "the Old Post Office" or Tafarn Sinc Preseli.

Suitable for: All

Note: All section of this walk not on Rights of Way are by permission of the Barony of Kemes. Please do nothing to abuse this permission or it may be withdrawn in future. All dogs on leads please.

Along the way

This walk passes beneath the disused and intriguing Rosebush Quarries following the old railway line before climbing via forestry tracks onto the prehistoric Golden Road and the highest point in West Wales with its Bronze Age cairns, returning via a green lane – an excellent spot for bilberry picking.

Ponies, buzzards and sheep are all to be seen, as well as a variety of birdlife. With the heather and gorse in bloom the hills are beautiful, while bilberrying will prolong interest and the time taken.

Tafarn Sinc Preseli – a famous historical local landmark – is worth a visit, as are the restaurant and tea rooms of the Old Post Office.

The Walk

From roadside parking by "the Old Post Office" or Tafarn Sinc Preseli, follow the track under the towering old quarries.

1. Go through a gate into the forest and follow the track for 250 metres before forking left over a stream and along a wide path below the forest. This path rejoins the track after 700 metres. Go straight on uphill. Bear left at the fork, then left again on a grassy ride up to the edge of the forest.

2. Turn right onto the prehistoric and often boggy "Golden Road", keeping the forest fence on your right as you climb.

3. Keep to the fence as it bears right and leads you to a stile onto the open hill. A clear, if winding path then leads you to the top of Foel Cwmcerwyn with its trig column and cairns.

4. A clear, if steep path leads down the far side of the hill. This crosses a somewhat boggy area to join a green lane running along the side of the forest.

5. Approximately one mile down this lane you will find a way-marked stile on your right. Cross this, pass a row of trees on your right to another stile. Follow the way-marks left onto a track which bears right downhill to a farm. Follow the farm track to the road. At the road turn right and after 50 metres you are back at the start.

Foel Cwm Cerwyn

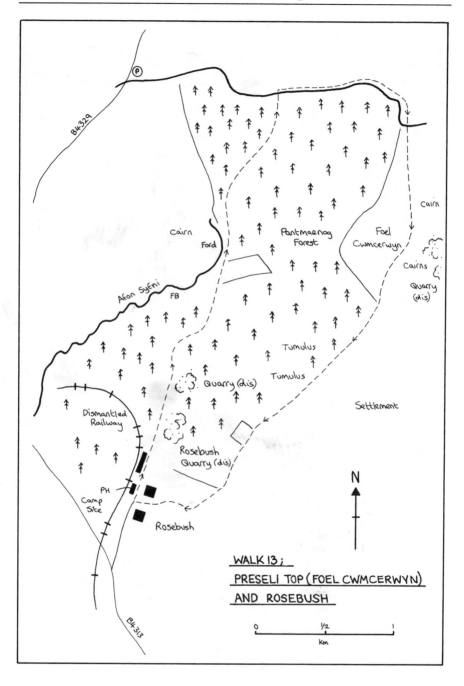

WALK 13;

PRESELI TOP (FOEL CWMCERWYN)

AND ROSEBUSH

14: History in the Preselis

Distance: 9 miles (14.5km)

Time: 4 hours

Maps: OS Landranger 145 Cardigan and surrounding area; OS Pathfinder 1033 Newport (Trefdraeth) and Eglwyswrw; OS Outdoor Leisure 35 North Pembrokeshire

Start: Roadside at Ref 165 330

Terrain: Easy hill walking, mainly on well-defined tracks. Muddy in places after rain.

Nearest town: Cardigan

Parking: Limited parking on grass verge at start

Refreshments: None

Stiles: 1

Suitable for: Children; dogs on leads

Note: Sections of this walk not on Rights of Way are used by permission of the Barony of Kemes. Please do nothing to abuse this permission or it may be withdrawn in future. All dogs on leads please.

Along the way

West Wales is thick with Celtic legends and prehistoric remains. The Preseli Mountains feature widely in Welsh legend and Arthurian connections abound in Pembrokeshire. Walking these hills conjures up Celtic twilight for those with imagination. Patrolled by buzzards, foxes, ponies and lambs, this is a wild and beautiful area.

This walk takes in two hill forts, the source of the Stonehenge Bluestones, a stone circle, two aircraft wrecks, several Bronze Age cairns and a prehistoric road, all linked by good upland walking with superior views.

Foel Drygarn, winter

The Walk

The walk starts by leaving the road by a rough track heading roughly north. After about 200 metres this takes you out onto the open hill via a gateway.

1. Join the obvious track that winds its way up onto the first summit of the day, Foel Drygarn. With over 200 hut circles, two stone walls and three Bronze Age cairns, Foel Drygarn is a wonderful example of an Iron Age fort and gives excellent views.

   From here descend southwards and take the path running across the heather to join the major track running along the length of the Preselis.

2. Turn west and follow this ancient route, with the intrusive modern forestry on your left. The path you are now on is an ancient road, used in prehistoric times to ferry Irish gold from its landing place at St David's to England, as well as by the Romans, the Flemish and by drovers. History under your feet.

   After about half a mile you come to some crags and outcrops. You can either continue on the path or move south into the rocks and follow them in a small loop, rejoining the path just north of Carn Menyn – the source of Stonehenge's Bluestones.

3. From here the main path can be rather boggy, so it is better to follow lesser paths further north by way of some unusual "tors" onto the top of the ridge before heading westward to Carn Bica with its Bronze Age cairn and the adjacent Bedd Arthur (Arthur's Grave) stone circle.

4. From Carn Bica head south-south-west along a broad ridge. After about half a mile start looking for the remains of an allied bomber that crashed during training in WW2. A few white posts help you find the site, with its memorial plaque. If you fail to find this awkward-to-locate memorial, drop off the west side of the ridge, descending to a good track that will lead you back up and over the main ridge at a natural pass.

5. In the valley to your left are the sites of Pembrokeshire's last glacier, ancient settlements and standing stones marking where

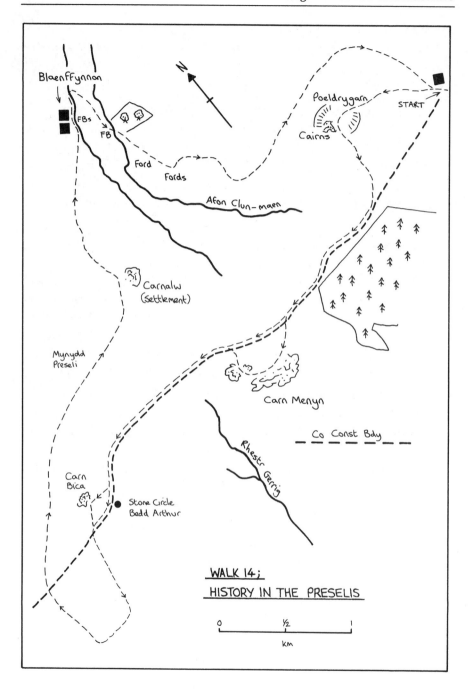

Blaenffynnon

FBs
FB
Ford
Fords
Afon Clun-maen

N

Poeldrygarn
Cairns
START

Carnalw
(Settlement)

Mynydd
Preseli

Carn Menyn

Co Const Bdy

Carn
Bica
Stone Circle
Bedd Arthur

Rhestr Gerrig

WALK 14;
HISTORY IN THE PRESELIS

0   ½   1

km

King Arthur's sons are said to have died. The summit to the west is Foel Cwmcerwyn, the highest point in West Wales, topped with Bronze Age cairns, while the rocks on the main ridge are said to be Arthur's knights killed and turned to stone by the Great Black Boar.

Descending the old drove road above Carn Goedog, look out for the remains of another wrecked aircraft as you follow this excellent path to Carnalw. This hill fort is built on a Rhyolite "tor" and features elaborate defences, including a "chevaux-de-frise" (stones laid to prevent horses or men charging up) inconsistent with its size.

6. Used during the filming of the BBC film "Tumbledown", Carnalw played the part of the Falkland Mountain and you can still find "military" rubbish, such as fired blanks, in the rocks.

Continue down the old drove road, turning right as you come to the wall above a very "posh" dwelling, and follow the sometimes wet path down to the road. Turn right and take the first track to the right where the road bears left after about 100 metres, and head uphill on a good path past various properties back onto the open hill.

As the path passes various houses its quality deteriorates, but although the ground is wet in places, as long as you follow roughly south-east with a wall and stream on your left, you will be OK.

After about a mile you come to the top of cultivated land. Turn left and follow the excellent track that swings round between Foel Drygarn and the farmland to take you past an old sheep dip back to the start of the walk.

15: Foel Drygarn and Foel Dyrch

Distance: 9 miles (14.5km)

Time: 5 hours

Maps: OS Landranger 145 Cardigan & Surrounding Area; OS Pathfinder 1033 Newport (Trefdraeth) & Eglwyswrw; OS Outdoor Leisure 35 North Pembrokeshire

Start: 165 330 track and road junction

Parking: Limited roadside parking

Terrain: Rough moorland and hill paths. Very wet and boggy in places, notably the bottom of the valley of the Eastern Cleddau.

Refreshments: None

Stiles: 6

Suitable for: All. Dogs on leads – sheep grazing

All parts of this route not on rights of way are by kind permission of the Barony of Kemes. Please do not abuse this permission or it may be withdrawn in future. All dogs on leads please.

Along the way

North Pembrokeshire is littered with prehistoric – and more recent – remains and this walk takes in Foel Drygarn, an Iron Age hill fort with three large Bronze Age cairns as well as many hut circles, passes close to standing stones, ancient cairns, a prehistoric burial chamber and the site from which were quarried the Stonehenge Bluestones. In addition it uses trackways, one of which – the Gold Road – runs along the crest of the Preseli Ridge. These were once used to transport items such as Irish gold from the coast to the heart of Britain, and are still regularly used today. The views afforded by this route are breathtakingly beautiful and, on a clear day, range

Foel Drygarn

from Snowdonia to the Brecon Beacons, with, it is said, possible glimpses of Devon and Ireland.

The Walk

1. From the start head up the rough track towards Foel Drygarn, crossing onto open land and taking the path that climbs the flank of this hill to gain its rock summit.

2. From the summit cairns head roughly south on narrow paths across the saddle, heading past the remains of Carn Ferched towards the forestry to join the "Gold Road", a wide track on the top of the ridge.

3. Turn right along this track past two rock outcrops, the second having a sheep-fold built against its northern face.

   Just past this sheep-fold bear left at a path junction and head for more outcrops. Follow this for 300 metres then drop left just beyond Carn Gyfrwy, down a steep bank headed for a cottage at the foot of the forestry.

This is a rough and somewhat boggy descent with little in the way of a path, but which brings you via the cottage's track onto a road.

4. Turn left and follow the road for 150 metres to just beyond a cottage (Glan-Rhyd) on your left and a ruinous barn on your right. You leave the road by a gate on your right and follow a stream-side path.

5. As the path opens into a field, take your line from the right-hand wall and cross the field (boggy) to a footbridge across the Eastern Cleddau River, here a small stream.

6. Cross the fence in front of you and follow the left side of the hedge as it runs up to a derelict cottage and turns into an attractive green lane.

   At a gate on your right 100 metres on from the cottage, look down to the far corner of the field and you will see two impressive standing stones.

7. Continue up the lane, go through a gate into a field, keeping to the left hedge to gain another green lane by the gate in the corner of the field.

   Follow this to the farmyard of Dolaumaen, where you climb up left to gain a surfaced lane. Turn right and follow the lane for about 900 metres where a way-marker points you left up a track.

   Where the track veers left again after 250 metres, turn right on a path that contours south-west to south around Foel Dyrch above the fencing, before slowly descending towards a farm.

   On reaching a gate at the corner of two fences, do not go through, but turn left; the path (way-marked in places) climbs above the fence to an old abandoned quarry.

8. From here the path drops slightly and passes two ruins before swinging north-east – always above the fence-line – and north to cross the ridge and descend to a gate in a wall. Do not go through the gate but turn right, passing through a gate in the corner where fences and wall meet.

9. Follow the way-marks down through two gateways, then swing

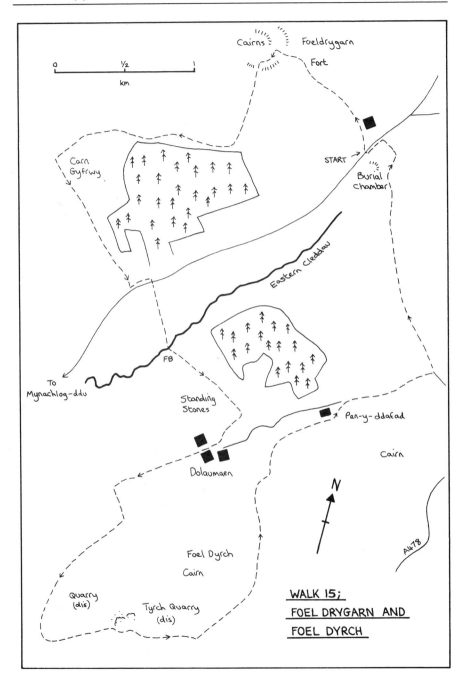

WALK 15;

FOEL DRYGARN AND

FOEL DYRCH

right and along the length of the field to a stile and hunters gate in the north-east corner.

From here, follow the path with the wall on your left up to a small farm, then along the farm track to a surfaced lane. Turn right and follow the lane for some 700 metres to the top of the bank.

10. Here the lane turns sharp right and our route goes left through a gate to follow an ancient track directed towards Foel Drygarn. At first fairly open, this track becomes a green lane before opening up into a field after about 1,200 metres.

11. Down to your left is an almost hidden prehistoric burial chamber.

Cross the field by the obvious path to the far corner where a short track leads you to the road.

Turn left to regain the start after 200 metres of road walking.

8. Turn left and follow the verge 500 metres back to the start.

16: Foel Drygarn and Carn Menyn

Distance: 3 miles (5km)

Time: 2 hours

Maps: OS Landranger 145 Cardigan and surrounding area; OS Pathfinder 1033 Newport (Trefdraeth) and Eglwyswrw; OS Outdoor Leisure 35 North Pembrokeshire

Nearest town: Crymych, 1½ miles.

Start: Road side, map reference 165 330

Terrain: Moorland studded with rock outcrops and good hill tracks.

Parking: Parking on a grassy verge opposite a rough lane at Start.

Suitable for: All

All sections of this walk not on Rights of Way are by permission of the Barony of Kemes. Please do nothing to abuse this permission or it may be withdrawn in future. All dogs on leads please.

Along the way

Foel Drygarn is an Iron Age fort with three Bronze Age cairns and obvious ruins of the ancient walls. Carn Menyn is reputedly the source of the Stonehenge bluestones, while the major track used on the return is the prehistoric trade route known as the Golden Road.

Ponies and buzzards haunt these hills, while crows and other birds are also seen. I have seen traces of foxes and badgers up here. The heather in bloom is a beautiful sight.

The Walk

Leave the road by a way-marked rough track and pass a stile/gate onto the open hill. Take the track straight on for 75 metres before following an indistinct path on your left that improves as it climbs the hill.

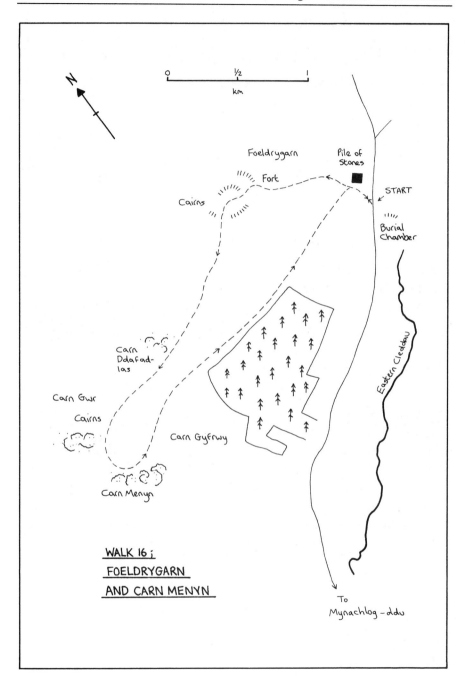

N

0   ½   1
km

Foeldrygarn   Pile of
                     Stones

Cairns   Fort   START

Carn
Ddafad-
las   Burial
                                       Chamber

Carn Gwr
Cairns   Carn Gyfrwy

Carn Menyn   Eastern Cleddau

WALK 16;
FOELDRYGARN
AND CARN MENYN

To
Mynachlog-ddu

1. The summit is well worth exploring before you cross and descend towards the nearest rock outcrop of Garn Ddu Fach.

2. Faint paths cross the streams to this point and continue on to the larger outcrop of Carn Dafad-Las. From here carry straight on for 500 metres before swinging left across pathless hillside to reach the imposing outcrops of Carn Menyn.

3. These fascinating rocks are well worth exploring before you return to the crest of the ridge and join the Golden Road which is then followed back to the start of the walk, keeping the main outcrops, forest and fence on your right.

Foel Drygarn

17: Strumble Head and Carregwastad Point

Distance: 10 miles (16km)

Time: 5 hours

Maps: OS Landranger 157 St David's and Haverfordwest area; OS Pathfinder sheet 1032 Fishguard (Abergwaun); OS Outdoor Leisure 35 North Pembrokeshire

Start: Strumble Head 894 411

Terrain: Coast Path. Good path but many steep but short, sections. Occasionally very close to cliff edge.

Inland: mainly good paths and green lanes.

Nearest town: Fishguard

Parking: Good parking at start

Refreshments: None

Stiles: 22-24 (one bad, some with lifting top bar)

Suitable for: Older children if kept under close supervision on cliffs. Dogs on leads.

Along the way

On Carregwastad Point there is a monument to the abortive French invasion of 1797. 1,200 of the sweepings of the French armed forces under an American (say no more!) landed on 22 February intent on raising the Welsh against England.

Due to poor leadership (see above), excessive drinking of (1) their brandy ration and (2) the shipwrecked wine from a nearby wreck, and the prompt action of the local yeomanry, it was all over by 4pm on 24 February when the invasion force surrendered on Goodwick sands. Legend would have it that the appearance of local ladies in

Strumble Head

red shawls and tall Welsh hats were taken for reinforcing "Red Coats" and the French were demoralised. It could be true – vast amounts of wine and brandy play havoc with the eyes! Total casualties: twenty dead Frenchmen, one dead Welsh woman – killed accidentally!

Strumble Head offers some of the finest walking along the beautiful Pembrokeshire Coast Path. With dramatic cliffs, deep coves and views along the coast in both directions, the walking is never boring and, in their seasons, you will find many wild flowers – some rare – including a great diversity of orchids. Keep your eyes open and you will see seals (young pups in the rocky coves in the autumn), dolphins, buzzards, peregrines, foxes and badgers among the varied fauna.

The Walk

1. From the car park at Strumble Head, with its fine views of the lighthouse (built in 1908) head east and get off the tarmac at a stile on the sharp corner. Following the well-maintained path makes navigation simple and you can concentrate your attention on the views. After about three-quarters of a mile you descend almost to sea level at Porth Sychan (be sure to turn left at the fingerpost) and this bay often holds a couple of the tamest seals I have ever seen, coming to within 15 feet of the pebble beach.

2. Climbing back up onto the cliff-tops the path takes you past the site of a Celtic saint's chapel and on past a wonderfully-sited cottage, Penrhyn, to Carregwastad Point with its monument to the French invasion. This part of the path is famous for the number and variety of orchids.

3. From Carregwastad Point continue along the Coast Path to the first stile. Cross this and leave the main path to follow an indistinct path roughly south-west over rocks and heather. After about a quarter of a mile you pass through a gateway into a well-maintained field. Follow the wall along the southern edge of the field and through a gate into a green lane.

4. This track eventually leads up through the charming farmyard

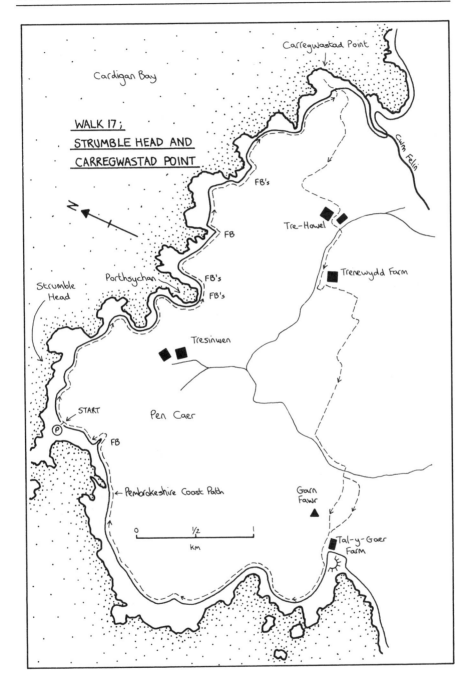

WALK 17;
STRUMBLE HEAD AND
CARREGWASTAD POINT

of Trehowel and up to the road. Trehowel was used as the French invaders' HQ and was where the surrender (according to some sources) was signed.

5. Turn right and follow this quiet back lane for about 500 metres, then turn left through a white gate with the name Trenewydd. Follow the good track past the stone cottages, then through a gate, past an old well and southward up the lane towards Garn Folch.

   At the top of the track turn left at a gate and pass through a much older-looking gate to gain the open hillside. Turn right here and follow the obvious and way-marked path that goes west, contouring under the craggy summits.

   Where the path enters a green lane through the ruins of a gate, turn left and follow the lane down to the tarmac road half a mile further on.

   Turn left at the road and follow it for half a mile to the car park below Garn Fawr (N.T.).

6. Turn right here and follow the path to the summit – an Iron Age hill fort and wartime look-out – for superb views. Those who do not like steep descents can backtrack 200 metres to a path that contours to the south of the hill, while others can head on along the obvious path to the west. Both reach Tal y Gaer farm where, by a footpath sign, you will find an almost invisible stone-roofed structure variously described as an Iron Age hut, a Celtic saint's cell and a mediaeval pig sty!

7. Follow the farm track down to the road where you regain the Coast Path. With some steep and rocky sections this will lead you back to Strumble Head past Porth Maen Melyn with its (private) stone cut stairs to the bay, wartime buildings and some wonderful views of the lighthouse.

18: Llanwnda and Carregwastad

Distance: 4 miles (6.5km)

Time: 2 hours

Maps: OS Landranger 157 St David's and Haverfordwest area; OS Pathfinder 1032 Sheet Fishguard; OS Outdoor Leisure 35 North Pembrokeshire

Start: Ref 932395 Llanwnda

Terrain: Green lanes and field paths, mostly well defined

Nearest town: Fishguard

Parking: Limited roadside parking at start

Refreshments: None

Stiles: 2

Suitable for: All

Along the way

This short figure-of-eight hike will especially appeal to those with an interest in history as it has a prehistoric burial chamber and standing stone, a stone circle, a Celtic style, Bellcote Church with five inscribed stones, four crosses, one Celtic face set into the wall, a holy well and the site of the last invasion of mainland Britain. Not bad for a four-mile walk!

The Walk

1. Leave your car on the roadside near the church by the village green with its boulder remains of a stone circle, and backtrack up the road for 150 metres, turning right up a narrow lane. By a white bungalow called "Garn Fach" this becomes a narrow grassy path winding up in the shadow of Carnwnda (N.T.) towards "Henner School" on the skyline. Before you reach this,

Llanwnda church

turn left just before crossing the boundary of the moorland
(where the path becomes a narrow lane) and, on a grassy path
towards the rocks.

2. To visit the burial chamber take a narrower path to your left
    above the obvious Bronze Age standing stone in the field to the
    south of the rocky outcrop. After about 100 metres of winding
    rocky path, a fork to the left, seemingly descending back to the
    white bungalow, will take you to the burial chamber. Retrace
    your footsteps to the main path, turn left and follow the obvious
    way-marking through a collection of houses and outbuildings
    back to the road. Turn left and you will soon be back at the village
    centre and stone circle.

3. Turn left here up the track signed "unsuitable for motors" and
    bear right at the track junction a little way beyond "Llanwnda
    House". Follow this sometimes muddy, sometimes surfaced lane
    for 1,200 metres past hedges full of a profusion of wild flowers.
    This lane called "Feidr Pont Eglwys" or "Church Bridge Road",
    is at least 1,000 years old and was once of great importance.

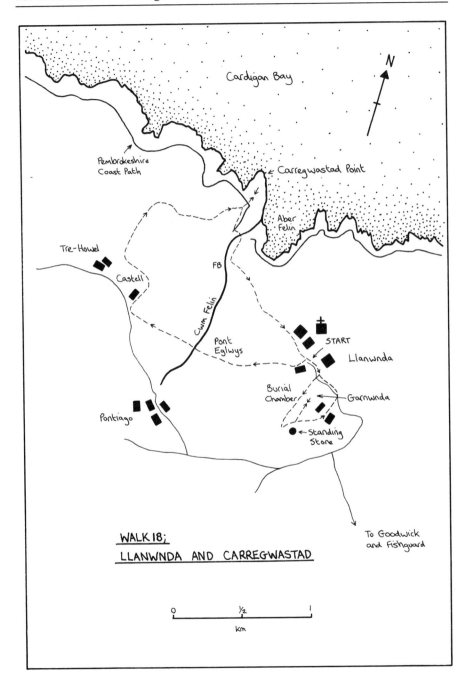

Cardigan Bay

N

Carregwastad Point

Pembrokeshire
Coast Path

Aber
Felin

Tre-Howel

FB

Castell

Cwm Felin

Pont
Eglwys

START

Llanwnda

Burial
Chamber

Garnwnda

Pontiago

Standing
Stone

WALK 18;
LLANWNDA AND CARREGWASTAD

To Goodwick
and Fishguard

0   ½   1

km

Reaching the end of the track you immediately turn off the road
you have reached, going right down the track to "Castell", an
imposing building set inside an ancient embankment, "Y Castell".

4. 200 metres after curving past the house, the track forks left to
   Tre-Howel, the French invaders' HQ and, some say, where they
   signed the surrender, and right, down a well-surfaced track
   towards the sea. Turn right and follow the track as it curves to
   the right, ignoring a side turning, and at the end take the left of
   two gates into a field.

   Follow the top of the field and take the left of two gateways into
   a very rough – almost moorland – field. A faint and confusing
   collection of paths and trods cross this, dropping north-east
   towards the Coast Path at the stile onto Carregwastad Point. Here
   you will find the memorial stone to the French Invasion in 1797.

5. On 22 February 1797 a ship, loaded with 1,500 of the lowest
   criminals and mercenaries fighting for the French, landed intent
   on marching through Wales and raising the principality against
   the rest of Britain.

   Ineptly led (by an American!), the troops got roaring drunk on
   their brandy ration and wine from a recent wreck and met
   hostility in the shape of the well-organised Pembroke Militia.

   Legend has it that the Welsh ladies in their red shawls and tall
   black hats who had come as spectators, were mistaken by the
   invaders to be a Redcoat regiment, adding to their demoralisa-
   tion.

   By the evening of 24 February the invasion force had surrendered
   with casualties totalling 20 – including 8 drowned – to the Welsh
   losses of one Welsh woman accidentally killed in a pub when a
   pistol went off during loading!

6 From the monument re-cross the stile and follow the Coast Path
   left, down into a delightful and unexpected deep dingle filled
   with the sound of stream and bird-song. Climbing up the other
   side you leave the coast with its stunning views, seals, dolphins,
   buzzards and all sorts of sea birds, and go through the way-

marked gate ahead. Follow the faint path almost parallel to the lip of the dingle inland to a gate at the far corner of the field. Here you pick up way-marks that lead you straight across the next field to a short section of green lane. At the far end of this follow the left edge of the field ahead round to a stile. Cross this onto a track and follow this to just before the buildings where a finger-post directs you up a grassy path to the right.

7. Just before crossing the stile back onto the green, on a fairly boggy section of path by a typical Pembrokeshire farmhouse (note the cemented roof), you will find the remains of a holy well, said to have healing properties, but often dry.

   Llanwnda was obviously spiritually important before Christianity came to the area, but the Church is worth a visit. The bell cote is in a dangerous state but walk around the church hunting the four incised stone (Celtic?) crosses set into the walls and the Celtic stone face that is in a less obvious setting.

   From Neolithic to Napoleonic, this short walk is a trip through time and not too demanding on the legs.

19: Porthgain and Abereiddy

Distance: 5 miles (8km)

Time: 2½ hours

Maps: OS Landranger 157 St David's and Haverfordwest area; OS Pathfinder 1032 Fishguard and 1055 St David's and Solva; OS Outdoor Leisure 35 North Pembrokeshire

Start: Car park at Porthgain, grid ref 815 325

Terrain: Coast path and field paths. Muddy in places.

Nearest town: St David's

Parking: See start

Refreshments: The Sloop Inn, Porthgain – an excellent pub well used to catering for walkers. No dogs. Van at Abereiddy in the holiday season (ices, drinks, sandwiches – and fresh fish!)

Stiles: 7: 2 are awkward

Suitable for: Children (keep under close supervision on cliff path as the edge is close, crumbly and high) Dogs on leads.

Along the way

The small village of Porthgain, and smaller Abereiddy, are relics of the intense quarrying industry that once thrived in this area. The ruins in Porthgain are the remains of hoppers for crushed stone, while the imposing building between the harbour and the car park is the old machinery shed, and above the village traces of railway tracks, quarries and buildings give a haunting and timeless air to the walk.

At Abereiddy the seaward side of the quarry was blown up to create "The Blue Lagoon" (N.T.), a safe haven for boats, and now a favoured spot for diving, playing in small craft and "rock hopping". The far end of the beach is famous for its graptolites fossils.

Abereiddy

The "Watch Tower" on the headland above the quarries is where tradition has it that the Quarry Directors' wives held Tea Parties or the Directors held Board meetings, while it could just be a "day-mark" to guide ships into the quarry.

The Church of St Rhian, just off route, was founded in the 5th century, while the tower has existed, most likely as a refuge from sea raiders, since the 13th century. Although most of the Church dates from the 1800s it has ancient interest in its Ogham Stone (indecipherable) and the Celtic cross on the west side of the tower.

This walk is a mixture of coast and farmland walking, in the main on well-maintained and way-marked paths. The ruins of old industry far from detracting from the walk add interest, while Abereiddy gives an extra point of interest to geologists and those wanting a safe swim. Look out for the wide variety of wildlife from peregrine falcons through to innumerable sea birds. Wild flowers abound in spring.

The Walk

1. From the car park walk back past Porthgain Row cottages (visit the art gallery later for information and paintings of Porthgain and area, including the story of how the village bought itself) to the fork in the road. Across the road from the cottages follow the finger post up the un-surfaced track to just past a hut where another finger post points the way over a footbridge and stile and up to a kissing gate into a field. Follow the left-hand (eastern) hedge for about 300 metres to another kissing gate, then over the stile in front of you – next to a wide gate – onto an un-surfaced track around the attractive complex of Felindre.

2. Follow the track right, southwards, to the road at Llanrhian, noting the two standing stones on your right, one in a field, the other on open ground by the road. Manor Farm and Llanrhian Church, with its unusual tower, are very attractive and worth more than a brief glance.

3. Turn right at the road junction and walk about 100 metres to the village sign by a gate. Ignore the gate and climb the steep and awkward steps by the sign over the wall into a field. Follow the left-hand hedge for about 500 metres, climbing a wired-up gate in a fence soon after entering the field – until you come down to a footbridge, steps and stile, all in poor but usable condition.

4. Cross these and then climb diagonally across the field to a good gate into a green lane that leads up to Portheiddy – a farm and holiday cottage complex of great charm – and the road.

5. Turn right at the road and after about 50 metres leave the tarmac for a way-marked path through a gate by a double garage and diagonally down to a stile in the far corner. Cross the stile and follow the path to the attractive cottages of Abereiddy.

6. After fossil hunting – visually only, remove nothing! – at the south side of the bay, cross to the north end and passing the cottages destroyed in a huge storm in 1938, follow the low path left, to explore "The Blue Lagoon" before climbing the steep slope – with steps – to view the old quarries from above. The "Watch Tower", now a listed building, can be reached by a rough and

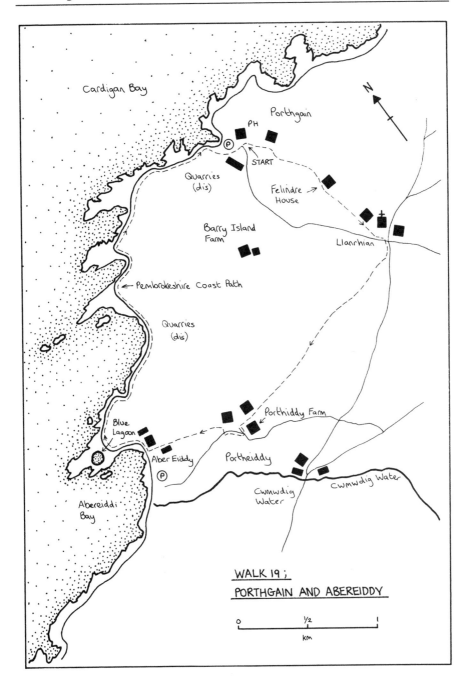

Cardigan Bay

Porthgain

PH

P

START

Quarries
(dis)

Felindre
House

Barry Island
Farm

Llanrhian

← Pembrokeshire Coast Path

Quarries
(dis)

Porthiddy Farm

Blue
Lagoon

Aber Eiddy

Portheiddy

P

Abereiddi
Bay

Cwmwdig
Water

Cwmwdig Water

WALK 19;
PORTHGAIN AND ABEREIDDY

0   ½   1
         km

steep path through part of the old workings where the headland joins the coast path.

7. The walk now follows the cliff path back to Porthgain, passing above deep coves and attractive beaches, and giving superb views and easy walking. Look out for seals and pups in the autumn. You can descend to the beach at Traeth-Llyfn by a long staircase, but remember, you will need to climb up again.

8. Approaching Porthgain you pass more evidence of quarrying with rail lines (followed for a while), tips and buildings visible, as well as the "daymarks" navigational aids to the ships coming to load up with stone in the harbour.

A final steep set of steps leads down from the cliff top to Porthgain harbour from where a stroll along the quayside under the old stone hoppers brings you back to the car park.

20: St David's Head and Penberry

Distance: 9 miles (14.5km)

Time: 5 hours

Maps: OS Landranger 157 St David's and Haverfordwest area; OS Pathfinder 1055 St David's (Ty Dewi) and Ramsey Island; OS Outdoor Leisure 35 North Pembrokeshire

Start: Whitesands Bay (Porth Mawr) car park, grid ref 734 271

Terrain: Mostly good paths, two steep climbs, one of which is very rocky (Carn Llidi). Muddy in places after rain

Nearest town: St David's

Parking: See start

Refreshments: Seasonal café at Whitesands

Stiles: 18 easy, 1 awkward

Suitable for: Older children; dogs (not on beach)

Along the way

As well as connections with St David and prehistory, wild life and wild flowers are notable along this section of the coast. Look out for seals, dolphins, buzzards, ravens, peregrines, choughs and a great variety of sea birds including razorbills, blackbacked gulls, shearwaters and stormy petrels. In the autumn look out for seal pups in the coves.

The coast and carns to the north of St David's city are rugged and beautiful and make wonderful walking. Add to this a good scattering of prehistoric remains, excellent views and charming local farms, and you will soon see why this is a favourite walk of mine.

Whitesands Bay from Carn LLidi

The Walk

1. Starting from Whitesands Bay, you soon find yourself walking through history. The beach itself was the terminus for an ancient gold road for shipping in Irish gold, as well as two Roman roads, and as you follow the Coast Path north from the car park you pass the site of a Celtic chapel (long gone) dedicated to St Patrick, who was a friend of St David.

2. The obvious and well-maintained path is followed out to the very tip of St David's Head (N.T.), itself an Iron Age promontory fort with three ditches known as Clawdd y Milwyr (Warriors Dyke), which held safe a settlement of which 8 hut circles can still be found. The views of the coast south of here, and of Ramsey Island are spectacular from the highest point of the fort.

   Following the Coast Path northwards for about 200 metres, you pass a Neolithic burial chamber dated to around 3,500 BC in an outcrop of rocks on your right.

3. Continuing north-east along the Coast Path, which follows the ridge of hard igneous rocks, look down into the valley to your right and you will make out the outlines of Iron Age fields and settlements below the slopes of Carn Llidi.

4. Keeping to the Coast Path, making sure to bear left when the path splits about one-third of a mile from the burial chamber, this obvious and well-used path is followed for about 3¼ miles to the shadow of the crags of Penberry. Children should be kept under strict control as the path often comes close to the edge of the high, sheer cliffs.

5. After a sharp pull up, you cross a stile under Carn Penberry (Penberi) and turn right along the fence to a second stile. Cross this and if you do not wish to sample the views from the summit, follow the path southward to Treleidir Farm. To reach the summit follow the way-mark "Ffoss y Mynach" (Monks Path) left at the stile, then bear right at a ruined wall, following faint paths. Descend to join the main route where you left it for this worthwhile diversion.

   The Ffos y Mynach is an ancient track that runs southwards from

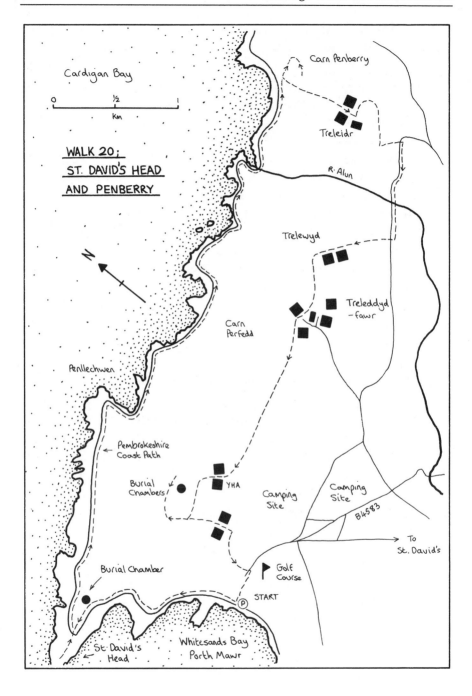

Cardigan Bay

0   ½   1
         Km

WALK 20;
ST. DAVID'S HEAD
AND PENBERRY

N

Carn Penberry

Treleidr

R. Alun

Trelewyd

Treleddyd
-fawr

Carn
Perfedd

Penllechwen

Pembrokeshire
Coast Path

Burial
Chambers   YHA

Camping
Site

Camping
Site

B4583

To
St. David's

Burial Chamber

Golf
Course

START
P

St. David's
Head

Whitesands Bay
Porth Mawr

Penberi to the other coast of the St David's promontory and was originally to delineate the land belonging to the church.

At Treleidir Farm take the surfaced road left out of the yard for about 300 metres before turning right into a green lane. This is another ancient route called Feidr Dwr (Water Street) and can be muddy after rain.

6. On reaching a tarmac lane, turn left, then at the junction, right. Follow this lane for about half a mile, then turn up a rough track to Trelewyd, a farm with some unusual outbuildings. Carry on past the farm, then when the path enters a field, turn left and follow a footpath (well-signed) into the unusual "farm cluster" of Treleddyd-Fawr.

7. Follow the footpath signs and zigzag through this attractive hamlet and gain an obvious and well-signed footpath to the Youth Hostel at Llaethdy. Turn right here and follow the track to bear left at a path junction, and contour under Carn Llidi.

Before descending through upper Porth Mawr, it would be criminal not to follow the track up Carn Llidi past remains of wartime look-outs, hydrophone and radar station and more Neolithic burial chambers. The final climb is a bit of a scramble, but worth the effort.

Descend to the road, turn right and you are soon back at your car. However, if the tide is right, an extra 1½ miles of beach strolling is an attractive bonus down the flat sands to Ogofgolchfa and back.

21: St David's Head

Distance: 3½ miles (5.5km)

Time: 2½ hours

Maps: OS Landranger 157 St David's and surrounding area; OS Pathfinder 1055 St David's and Solva; OS Outdoor Leisure 35 North Pembrokeshire

Nearest refreshments: Beach café, Whitesands car park (seasonal).

Start: Whitesands car park, map reference 734 271

Terrain: Cliff path and rough grazing. Moderate walking with some rough ground. The optional detour to the summit of Carn Llidi involves some rough scrambling.

Parking: See Start

Suitable for: All

Along the way

Ancient history is the rule here. Whitesands Bay was the terminus of a Bronze Age trade route between Ireland and Salisbury Plain and St Patrick left from here on his final trip to Ireland. A chapel once stood by the path.

The valley between Carn Llidi and the fort on St David's Head shows evidence of ancient field systems. St David's Head itself has the ruins of a massive wall system called "Warriors Dyke" and the remains of eight hut circles, while nearby is a Neolithic burial chamber or cromlech called Coetan Arthur. Other cromlechs are to be found by the remains of the radar and hydrophone stations – which are of a much later date!

Look out for seals and dolphins in the water, while the air is full of sea-birds such as cormorants, shearwaters and kittiwakes. Heather, bracken and gorse dominate the land.

Cromlech, St David's Head

The Walk

1. Take the Coast Path north from Whitesands car park and follow it to St David's Head fort.

2. Follow the obvious path from here going north-eastwards to Coetan Arthur and on for just under a mile where a track joins the Coast Path from the right.

3. Follow this south-westward down the valley under Carn Llidi with the ancient field systems (just visible) on your left.

4. After about half a mile bear left up a track that climbs up towards Carn Llidi and more cromlechs and the optional scramble to the summit.

5. Follow the rough track back down the hill through a farm to the road and the car park.

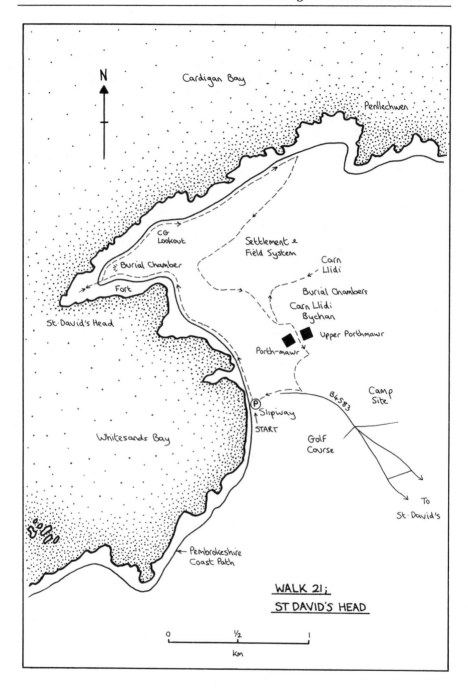

N

Cardigan Bay

Penllechwen

CG
Lookout

Settlement &
Field System

Carn
Llidi

Burial Chamber

Burial Chambers

Carn Llidi
Bychan

Fort

St·David's Head

Upper Porthmawr

Porth-mawr

Camp
Site

B4583

P
Slipway
START

Whitesands Bay

Golf
Course

To
St·David's

Pembrokeshire
Coast Path

WALK 21;
ST DAVID'S HEAD

0   ½   1
          Km

22: In and around St David's

Distance: 6 miles (9.5km)

Time: 3 hours

Maps: OS Landranger 157 St David's and Haverfordwest area; OS Pathfinder 1055 St David's and Ramsey Island; OS Outdoor Leisure 35 North Pembrokeshire

Start: Grove Car Park, Grid Ref 756 252

Terrain: Coastal path, field paths, muddy in places. Minor roads.

Nearest town: St David's

Parking: See Start, also alternative start at Porthclais Harbour

Refreshments: Many cafés in St David's

Stiles: 12 easy stiles and 1 awkward one, total 13.

Suitable for: Children, dogs.

Along the way

St David's Cathedral, Bishop's Palace (ruin) and Cathedral close. St David's Cathedral is smaller than most English cathedrals, but has an unrivalled position in its valley. Started by Bishop Peter de Leia in 1181 on the site of earlier buildings, the Cathedral is well worth an extended visit in its own right. Look for the "green men" – pre-Christian symbols – incorporated into the decoration.

Next to the Cathedral are the ruins of the Bishop's Palace. This was probably the most splendid in Britain, reflecting the great importance of St David's. The Palace, mainly built between 1328 and 1347 by Bishop Gower, is also worth a visit and is a calm and relaxing place to sit after the walk. 'Phone the Dean of St David's Cathedral on 01437 720202 for details of forthcoming events, or for information on the Bishop's Palace call CADW – Welsh historic monuments – on St David's 720517.

Porth Clais harbour

St David's is Britain's smallest city and is smaller than some villages. At one time it was extremely important as a site of pilgrimage and although now a major tourist centre, the City is quiet and peaceful, especially out of season. Although the coast forms part of the Pembrokeshire Coast Path and is very popular with walkers and climbers, inland paths are very quiet – as are the back lanes. Despite this the paths are well-marked and in good condition, making this a very pleasant walk.

The Walk

1. From the car park cross the A487 (St David's to Haverfordwest road) and turning right, then immediately left onto a quiet country lane. Follow this for about 100 metres before turning left down a narrow but well-maintained footpath between two hedges.

   After about 100 metres this becomes a surfaced lane serving a few cottages before crossing New Street and passing down beside the small Catholic Church to come out on Nun Street. Turn right here and after about 50 metres cross over and take the little lane with an easily missed wooden sign "St David's City Walk" pointing down to a view of Carn Llidi.

   A little way along here, go through the way-marked gate and follow the obvious track northwards. Crossing a stile, this becomes a winding path set between hedges. Follow this until you come, after about one-third of a mile, to a slightly wider cross path where you are faced by a metal gate. This track is an old Pilgrim road called Meidr Dwyll. Turn left here and follow this green lane down to Pont y Penyd Bridge through a wooded valley. Cross the bridge and follow the road down into the Cathedral close.

2. When you reach the ruins of the Bishop's Palace, turn right up a rough lane to a minor road. Turn left and follow this road south-west. At the road junction turn right, then left, signed St Justinian's, then Treginnis, passing Parc y Castell on your left, reputed to be either the first settlement at St David's or a Norman fort.

3. Just over the bridge turn left, passing a house "Nant y Felin" and following a rough track down to the old mill. Cross the stream and bear left up to a wooden gate that brings you onto a green lane, "Ffordd Melin Isaf" (little mill road) that at first follows the mill race, then gently climbs up to a road.

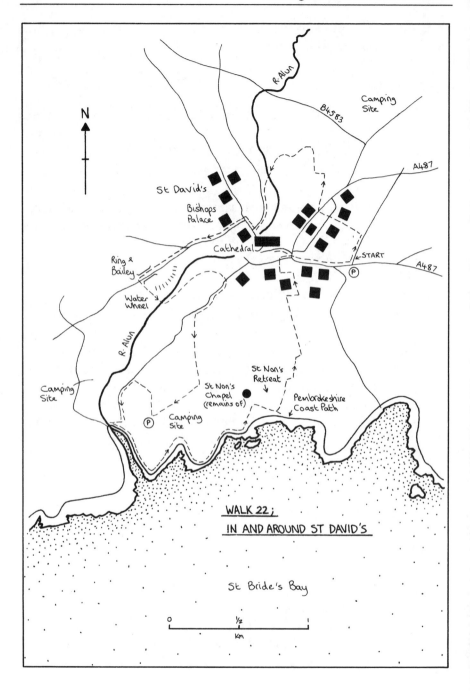

N

St David's
Bishops
Palace

Cathedral

Ring &
Bailey

Water
Wheel

R. Alun

R. Alun

B4583

Camping
Site

A487

START

A487

P

Camping
Site

P

Camping
Site

St Non's
Chapel
(remains of)

St Non's
Retreat

Pembrokeshire
Coast Path

WALK 22;

IN AND AROUND ST DAVID'S

St Bride's Bay

0   ½
         km

Turn right, then a little way past "Lower Moor Nurseries" leave the tarmac up a track to your left with a finger post marked "St David's City Walk".

Follow the obvious path over Waun Isaf Moor (N.T.) (duckboards are positioned at boggiest places). At the first stile go straight on and come to an awkward stile into a narrow walled lane. Turn right and cross another stile into a field. Make for the farm buildings – crossing two more stiles. Turn right onto the farm drive. This takes you to the road which leads to the attractive harbour "Pôrth Clais" (N.T.) that was so important to St David's and which features strongly in Welsh legend.

4. Do not cross the bridge – but do note the slate slab pedestrian bridge. Turn left and climb above the lime kilns where lime for agriculture and for building was produced by burning imported limestone, and gain the cliffs of the Coast Path.

5. Follow the Coast Path for three-quarters of a mile past cliffs enjoyed by rock climbers, until you come to a gap in the landward wall with a path leading up to the ruins of St Non's Chapel and well. St Non was St David's mother and St David was born here, the well springing up at his birth. The spring is said to have curative powers and is littered with coins offered by sufferers wanting a cure for various ailments.

The path past the well rejoins the Coast Path below the modern monastery and almost immediately our route cuts inland up a well-marked path, Ffordd Aaron (Aaron's road) signposted to St David's.

6. This path brings you back to the outskirts of St David's behind modern housing. Turn right then left onto a road with a finger post "St David's". Follow the road to a T-junction, turn left then right, right again then left and you will find yourself overlooking St David's Cathedral.

To regain the start of the walk, turn back up past the market cross and follow the road for one-third of a mile back to the car park past most of St David's shops.

23: Treffgarne and Plumstone Mountain

Distance: 11 miles (18km)

Time: 5 hours

Maps: OS Landranger 157 St David's and Haverfordwest area; OS Pathfinder Sheet 1056 St David's and Solva; OS Outdoor Leisure 35 North Pembrokeshire

Start: Parking 500 metres north of Nant y Coy Mill on the A40 Haverfordwest to Fishguard Road, map reference 954 256

Terrain: Mostly good paths and tracks – 2½ miles road walking on quiet lanes. Muddy in places.

Nearest town: Haverfordwest

Parking: More parking at Nant y Coy Mill 953251.

Refreshments: Nant y Coy Mill, "Milking Parlour" Tea Room, home-made cakes.

Stiles: 18, most in excellent condition.

Suitable for: Children and dogs on leads

Along the way

Treffgarne and Plumstone Mountains feature imposing outcrops of volcanic rock which rise suddenly from moorland, dominating the area and its prehistoric remains. Much of the walking is on old tracks and "green lanes" that were once of much local importance.

Place names on this walk are interesting and you will pass the ruins of "Step Inn", "Start Naked" and "Gwachal Tagy" roughly translated as "beware of strangling".

This walk offers wonderful views both of and from the rock outcrops of Poll Carn, Plumstone Mountain and Maiden Castle. The last two offer interesting places to stop for lunch or tea as they offer views from shelter. On a good day you can even make out Ireland, while closer are the Preselis and Milford Haven. Much of the walk is way-marked, but in places the route here follows un-waymarked paths, so do not blindly follow the arrows!

Plumstone Rock and Plumstone Mountain

The Walk

1. From the parking area, following way-marks, the walk heads south parallel to the main road on a farm lane, but soon curves away past a building and heads westward. Now on a rough track the route continues for 500 metres going round the north side of farm buildings and through a metal gate onto another un-surfaced lane. Follow this track for 300 metres to where the obvious path descends into the valley. Leave the track here and follow the way-mark that points slightly uphill to the north-west.

2. A faint trod curves you past an ancient settlement up to the top corner of the field and an excellent stile into the next field. Leave this field immediately by another stile on your left which puts you onto an almost dead straight path to Brimaston. Simply follow the way-marks and keep the field boundaries on your left, then as the path turns into a green lane, follow this.

3. After a mile you come to a T-junction of green lanes. Turn right here. Beware of the gate as it is merely propped up. Turn left, then after a couple of metres turn right on the left of a bank and go through the obvious gate (one hinge only) and past a converted chapel up to the road.

   Turn left and follow this lane for 1 mile down to the B4330 where you turn left to road-walk a further half a mile up to the crest of the hill.

4. At the top of the hill turn right along a way-marked and gated lane heading for the obvious outcrop of Plumstone Rock. This makes an excellent place for a rest before heading off along the way-marked path, roughly westward past tumuli and across two fences, for 650 metres, then north-west down a fenced path for 500 metres to near the ruins of Step Inn.

5. Follow the way-marked path south-west for 1,000 metres from here, diagonally across the first of two fields then on the same line across the second to the ruinous "Start Naked", then climb southwards along the boundary on your left until after about 500 metres you come to the forestry plantation. Cross the fence onto

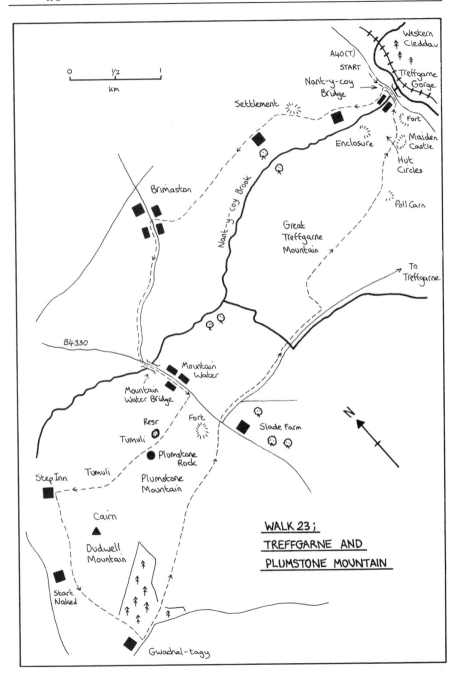

WALK 23;

TREFFGARNE AND

PLUMSTONE MOUNTAIN

the forestry track and follow this south for 400 metres to the road at Gwachal Tagy.

6. Turn left here and after 100 metres leave the road for the way-marked forestry track. After following this path through and out of the woods follow the grassy track straight on when the main track swings left. On reaching open moorland follow the main track for about 300 metres then drop right to a boundary wall. Keeping this on your right follow narrower tracks across the moor, across a field to the lower right corner, then into a lane.

7. This ancient through route brings you below an Iron Age "Rath" to the B4330, at "Ladies' Cross".

   Cross over and follow the lane signposted to Treffgarne for about 1¼ miles and to the third lane off to your left (north). This one has both a dead-end sign and a way-mark and there is a barn on the corner.

8. Follow this lane uphill for 300 metres then fork right, signposted to Lower North Hill. After about 150 metres go through the way-marked gate on your right. The path now heads east-north-east, climbing over Great Treffgarne Mountain and down towards Poll Carn. Keep the boundary on your right until you are immediately above the farm, then cross a stile and drop in a more northerly direction diagonally across the field down to the stile into the common ground around the rugged outcrop of Maiden Castle.

9. The views from this outcrop are superb and it makes an excellent rest point before continuing down past barely visible hut circles into Treffgarne Gorge by Nant y Coy Mill. The rocks on your right hold the remains of an ancient fort while the woods across the gorge hide the remains of Brunel's railway line, work on the building of which, ceased in 1851 due to the Irish potato famine. From the Mill you have a short walk on the grass verge of the A40 back to the start of the walk.

24: Plumstone Mountain

Distance: 3½ miles (5.5km)

Time: 2 hours

Maps: OS Landranger 157 St David's and Haverfordwest area; OS Pathfinder 1056 Newgale and Wolf's Castle; OS Outdoor Leisure 35 North Pembrokeshire

Nearest town: Haverfordwest

Start: Plumstone Rock is easily seen about 6 miles north of Haverfordwest on the B4330. map reference 924 235

Terrain: Tracks and field paths. Can be muddy in places.

Parking: There is limited roadside parking at the end of a reservoir road at the crest of the hill. Do not block any gateways.

Suitable for: All

Along the way

Superb views from most of the walk from the Preseli Hills to St David's, Milford Haven to Ireland (on a clear day). Ancient tracks cross the hill, Bronze Age tumuli are found near the summit, and an Iron Age fort can be seen to the south-west of Plumstone Rock itself.

As well as Plumstone Rock, other strange place names on the route include Step Inn (ruin), Start Naked (semi-ruined farm) and Gwachal Tagy, which translates as Beware of Strangling!

Welsh gorse, heather, tormentil, milkwort, foxgloves, meadowsweet and the Tenby daffodil can all be seen. Bird life includes skylarks, shorteared owls, hen harriers, buzzards, goldcrests and tree creepers. Look out for adders and lizards.

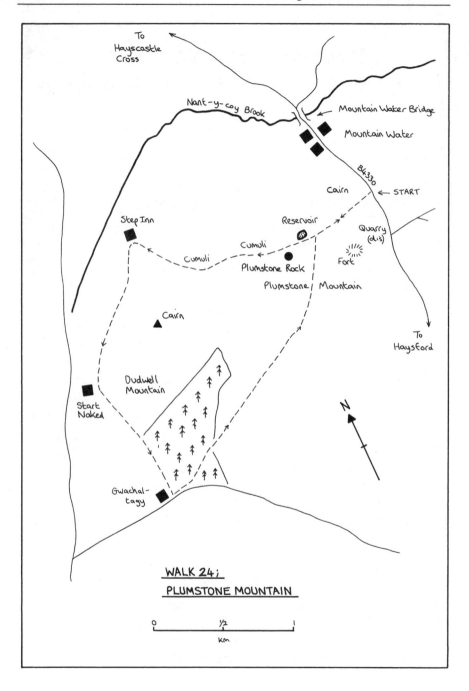

To
Hayscastle
Cross

Nant-y-coy Brook

Mountain Water Bridge

Mountain Water

B4330

Cairn   ← START

Step Inn

Reservoir

Quarry
(dis)

Cumuli

Cumuli

Plumstone Rock

Fort

Plumstone Mountain

To
Haysford

Cairn

Dudwell
Mountain

N

Start
Naked

Gwachal-
tagy

WALK 24;

PLUMSTONE MOUNTAIN

0   ½   1

km

The Walk

1. From your car, walk up the reservoir road heading for the obvious outcrop of Plumstone Rock.

2. After examining this feature, follow the track to a stile. Cross this and reach the Bronze Age tumuli ahead. Cross the stile behind this and bear half-left to gain a track between two fences that leads down towards "Step Inn".

3. Just after some ruins on your right, turn left through a stile/gate and cross the field diagonally to a gate/stile. Continue in the same direction and cross a stile by Start Naked.

4. Turn left and follow the fence up over the hill as far as the corner of the forestry plantation. Cross a stile onto the forestry track down to "Gwachal Tagy".

5. Turn left on the road then go straight on along the forestry track into and beyond the trees for 600 metres onto open moorland.

An obvious path leads up below Plumstone Rock to the reservoir. Return to the start by the reservoir road.

"Start Naked"

25: Great Treffgarne Mountain

Distance: 4¼ miles (7km)

Time: 2 hours

Maps: OS Landranger 157 St David's and surrounding area; OS Pathfinder 1056 Newgale and Wolf's Castle; OS Outdoor Leisure 35 North Pembrokeshire

Nearest refreshments: Nant-y-Coy Mill

Start: Lay-by, map reference 954 256

Terrain: Good tracks, field paths and moorland. Can be muddy in places.

Parking: Park in the lay-by half a mile south of Wolf's Castle, 800 metres north of Nant-y-Coy Mill, on the A40 Fishguard to Haverfordwest Road.

Suitable for: All

Along the way

This walk takes in pleasant rural scenery before descending from Great Treffgarne Mountain by way of the impressive rock outcrops of Poll Carn and Maiden Castle. Excellent views over the region. Flag iris, gorse, heather and moorland flowers abound, while ravens, peregrines and buzzards are to be seen, especially around the rocks.

The Walk

1. Leave the lay-by by the track up to West Ford Farm. Skirt round the right-hand side of the farm buildings to pick up the green lane on the other side.

2. Where the lane dips into the valley, follow the way-marked path to the right that climbs up under an ancient settlement to a stile in the top corner of the field. Cross this, then another immediately on your left.

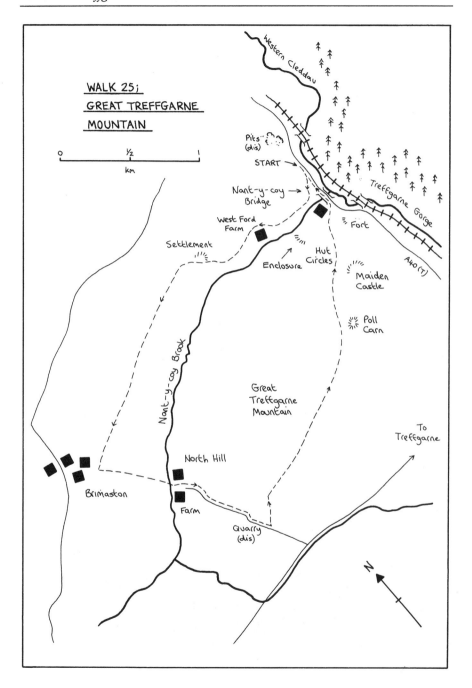

WALK 25;
GREAT TREFFGARNE
MOUNTAIN

0 ½ 1
km

Western Cleddau

Pits (dis)

START

Nant-y-coy Bridge

West Ford Farm

Settlement

Fort

Treffgarne Gorge

A40 (T)

Enclosure

Hut Circles

Maiden Castle

Poll Carn

Nant-y-coy Brook

Great Treffgarne Mountain

To Treffgarne

North Hill

Brimaston

Farm

Quarry (dis)

N

3. From here to Brimaston you go in almost a straight line for about 1 mile, at first keeping field boundaries on your left, then by a green lane.

4. When you come to a T-junction of tracks, turn left and follow the new path down to Nant-y-Coy Brook. Cross the streams and climb up through "North Hill" and follow the track uphill.

5. Just over the crest of the hill, turn left on a track signed to Lower North Hill. Just before the "private road" sign, cross the way-marked stile on your right and cross the field to the corner of the fences.

    Keep the fence on your right as you climb over Great Treffgarne Mountain and descend towards the rocks of Poll Carn.

6. Bear left diagonally down the field by Poll Carn.

7. Cross a stile into the common by the rocks of Maiden Castle before descending to the A40 by Nant-y-Coy Mill.

8. Turn left and follow the grass verge for 500 metres back to the start.

Maiden Castle

26: Nolton Haven

Distance: two walks of 2 miles (3.25km) each, or one of about 4 miles (6.5km)

Time: For the full walk – 2 hours

Maps: OS Landranger 157 St. David's and Haverfordwest; OS Pathfinder 1079 Haverfordwest; OS Outdoor Leisure 36 South Pembrokeshire

Start: Nolton Haven 860 186

Terrain: Cliff paths, field paths and quiet lanes

Refreshments: Mariners Inn, Nolton Haven

Nearest town: Haverfordwest

Parking: See start

Stiles: 5

Suitable for: Children – should be kept under control on the cliff sections.

Along the way

This walk boasts superb coastal scenery and views across St Brides Bay. Cliffs, caves and arches and the ruins of an old colliery – closed in 1905 – provide an interesting and only moderately difficult walk. The metaled road walked is on the line of the old Pilgrims Route to St David's while Nolton Haven has been used by smugglers and coal exporters in the past, but is now quiet and peaceful.

The Walk

1. From the Pembrokeshire National Park car park turn left up the road alongside the Mariners Inn. Turn right at the T-junction above the United Reform Church and, ignoring the Coast Path signs, follow the lane for 1 mile to Druidston Haven (not named after a Druid, but a Norman called Drue).

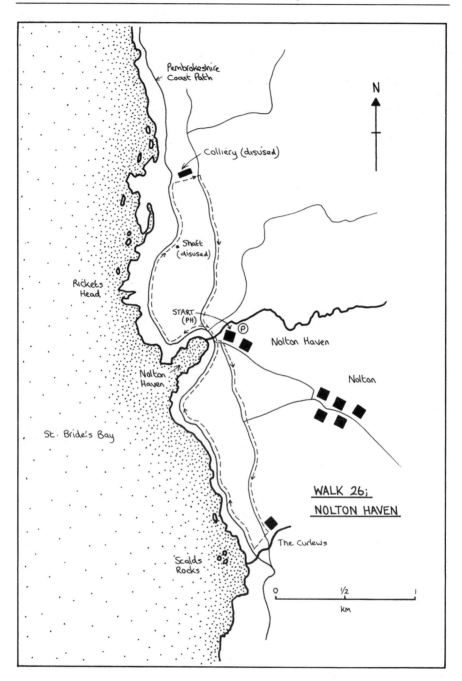

2. Here, just before crossing the stream and opposite a stone wall, take the path towards the sea.

3. Before reaching the beach you join the Pembrokeshire Coast Path and turn right up a flight of steps to gain the cliff top. Follow the path past caves etc, eventually descending into Nolton Haven by the weather-worn United Reform Church.

4. Go down left and cross the top of the beach, following Coast Path signs and follow the Coast Path up to Rickets Head.

   Here the path climbs to the top of the bank on your right (way-marked) and passes evidence of coal mining.

5. Eventually you come to the stone and brick ruins of the old colliery . Before descending to this the route turns right along the top of the slope (way-marked) and passes a pond before reaching the road. Cross onto the road, turn right and follow it back down to Nolton Haven.

Ruins of colliery near Norton Haven

27: Llawhaden

Distance: 6½ miles (10.5km)

Time: 4 hours – Allow extra for exploring the castle, church, hospice and ancient camp.

Maps: OS Landranger 158 Tenby; OS Pathfinder 1080 Narberth; OS Outdoor Leisure 36 South Pembrokeshire

Start: 070 173 Llawhaden Village, parking by picnic spot

Terrain: Mainly well way-marked riverside and woodland paths. Can be muddy in places. Superb views.

Nearest town: Narberth

Parking: See Start, or alternative start at village hall at 066 173.

Refreshments: Village shop and Information Centre (closed Tuesday and Saturday afternoons and all day Sunday). Village teas in Village Hall by Hospice (often closed out of season and on week days).

Stiles: 22

Suitable for: All. Dogs on leads through fields with livestock and farmyard.

Along the way

Once rivalling St David's in ecclesiastic power, Llawhaden Parish has a higher concentration of prehistoric sites than anywhere else in West Wales. Evidence has been found to show settlements in the parish from 1200 BC, Roman occupation, Celtic forts, a Norman Castle and mediaeval Hospice, a pilgrim route, drove roads and many other sites.

The village of Llawhaden was founded along with the Norman Castle, while the church that gives the village its name (Llawhaden = Church of Aidan) was built in the 13th century on an older site and incorporates an early Christian monument in the east wall.

Pont Gelli bridge

Although the church was re-built in the 19th century, it is still very attractive with its Pembrokeshire crenellated tower.

The village was re-founded in the 16th century by the Skyrme family, and in the 17th century was a hotbed of nonconformity. Today it is a sleepy village that makes an ideal base for exploring the beautiful surroundings of the Eastern Cleddau valley.

Look out for buzzards, kingfishers, flag iris, woodruff, orchids, ransoms and other flowers and birds.

The Walk

1. After reading the interpretation board by the picnic site, head for the Castle which is well worth a short detour. If locked, the keys are available from the shop. Before reaching the ruins you can drop down to the right, taking a narrow path beside a house called Oaklands, through Churchill Woods ancient woodlands, and steeply down to the road by the Church.

2. Turn right here and follow the quiet lane to the bridge over the Eastern Cleddau River. Cross over this ancient bridge and turn left, leaving the road just after it turns right and taking a step stile into the riverside field.

   The well way-marked path can be muddy in places as it follows the river for the next 1½ miles through fields and ancient coppiced woodlands containing masses of wild flowers, but does have board-walks in the worst places.

3. The route leaves the river to skirt a small disused quarry (be sure to take a left turn up a way-marked but narrow trod off the wide track from the quarry) and climbs above the woods, keeping to the field's left fence.

   After about half a mile the route leaves the wood edge and climbs diagonally from a well way-marked stile and across the field to the far hedge. You then go north keeping the hedge on your right.

   Do not follow the track into the farmyard, but take a stile to the left of the track and follow the hedge line on your right round the farm and down to a stile onto the quiet B 4313.

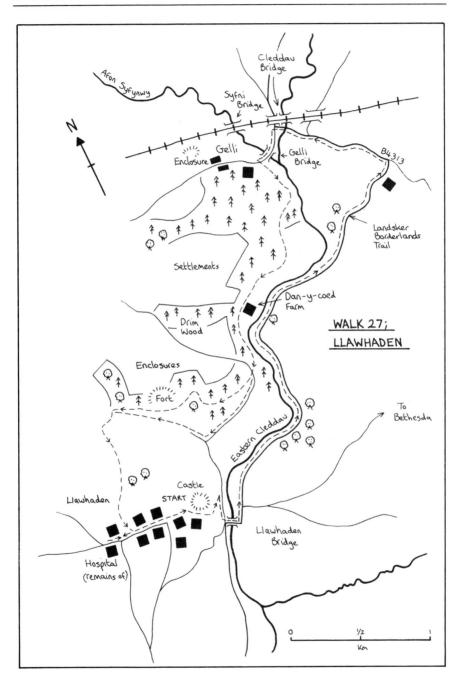

4. Turn left and follow the road down to a junction. Take the left fork signposted to Penffordd, cross the river by an old bridge and turn left – signposted to Llawhaden – and cross the ancient and unusual bridge at Pont Gelli.

5. Between the bridge and the 18th century Chapel take the way-marked bridleway up into the woods and follow an excellent track that winds through the trees.

   After about half a mile the track bends west and comes to a track junction. Turn left and left again, keeping to the lowest track.

6. At a junction three-quarters of a mile further on, turn right and follow the bridleway through Dan y Coed Farm and up to a road.

   Cross the road and go through a gate into an area of cleared woodland, and follow the track signposted "Holgan Camp".

7. After about half a mile along this track a second sign points up a narrow trod with steps up to the overgrown remains of this ancient promontory fort. Although little is visible other than two banks and ditches at the west end of the fort, it is worth a diversion before returning to the track and continuing west-wards.

   The track eventually leads down to a footbridge over a stream, which you cross to join an old drove road back to Llawhaden. Beware of the dogs at the first cottage, if they are still in residence; they went for my dog rather viciously.

8. On reaching the road in Llawhaden it is worth visiting the restored Hospice where there are extensive interpretation boards, a playground and the village hall tearoom and toilets, plus extra parking facilities.

9. Return eastwards to the start along the village road.

28: Llawhaden and Canaston Woods

Distance: 8 miles (13km)

Time: 4 hours. Allow extra for visiting Llawhaden Castle and Blackpool Mill.

Maps: OS Landranger 158 Tenby; OS Pathfinder 1080 Narberth; OS Outdoor Leisure 36 South Pembrokeshire

Start: 070173 Llawhaden Village. Parking by picnic spot.

Terrain: Mainly well way-marked field and woodland paths. Can be muddy in places.

Nearest town: Narberth

Parking: See Start

Refreshments: Blackpool Mill café/shop at Robeston Wathen

Stiles: 12

Suitable for: All. Dogs on leads on farmland.

The look-out at Blackpool Mill gates

Along the way

Llawhaden once rivalled St David's for ecclesiastic power and has a Norman Castle, Mediaeval Hospice, a fine church with a very attractive Pembrokeshire crenellated tower, and is situated on a prominent hill dominating an old pilgrim route.

Blackpool Mill is situated on the Eastern Cleddau and is on the site of earlier mills first referred to in 1555, and including a 16th century iron forge. The Mill now houses an exhibition of the old milling processes and machinery etc, while the old cellars have been converted to give a series of "caves" illustrating extinct prehistoric wild animals once found in this area – bears, hyenas, boar and reindeer – as well as the famous Welsh Red Dragon. Well worth visiting, Blackpool Mill has a good café and gift shop.

The Walk

1. After examining the interpretation board by the picnic site, head for the Castle (worth a detour) but before reaching the ruins take the path beside a house called Oaklands, down through Churchill Woods (ancient woodlands) to the road by the church.

2. Turn right here and follow the quiet lane to Llawhaden Bridge, an imposing stone structure. Do not cross the bridge but go straight on for 100 metres up the road to a gate just before the cottage called Gate-house/Ty Gat.

   Go through the gate and down the track. After passing through two more gates, below a deserted house, leave the track and bear right, avoiding a descent into a wet field, and cross a stile and hunter's gate to follow a good footpath at the bottom of a wooded bank.

   This leads into a farmyard after about 400 metres. Turn right up the drive, then turn left after about 50 metres following waymarks between an old and a newer barn.

   Go through a gate onto a rough track then through the first gate on your left into fields. A narrow trod crosses the centre of the field without losing height and through several more gates and fields down onto a metaled drive which takes you to the main road just west of Canaston Bridge.

3. Cross the road with care and turn right following the verge for 300 metres before turning left into Slebech Woods, just after a smaller bridge, and follow a broad forestry track through the trees for three-quarters of a mile. At the track junction at the foot

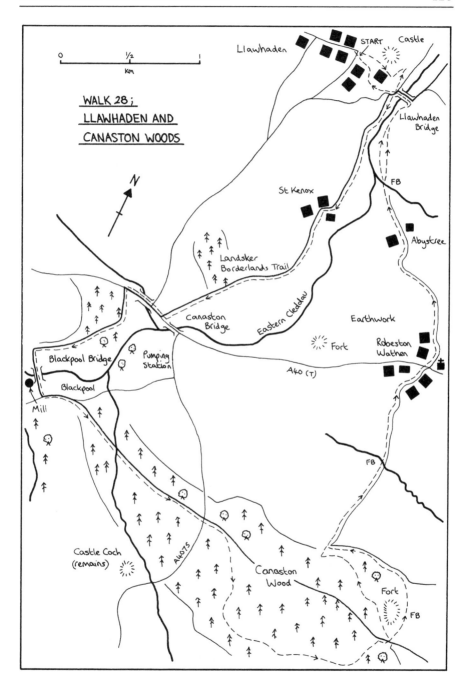

WALK 28 ;
LLAWHADEN AND
CANASTON WOODS

of the slope turn left and cross two bridges over a leat and the Eastern Cleddau to Blackpool Mill.

4. From the mill follow the drive to the road. Turn left and follow the road for 100 metres, then turn right up the woodland track way-marked "The Knights' Way". Follow this for about 1 mile before crossing the A4075 into Canaston Woods.

5. Go straight on along the broad track for 100 metres before turning right up a track that soon becomes a narrow way-marked path through the trees.

   At the first way-marked path junction – after half a mile – turn left and follow this path for three-quarters of a mile, crossing a path cross-roads and a stony track before descending back onto the "Knights' Way", now a sunken lane. Turn right, then after 50 metres turn left up a narrow track.

   50 metres on, you can turn left or right. The right fork takes you down to Valley Road more directly (turn left when you reach this quiet lane) while turning left takes you through more woodland to a path junction where you turn right to gain Valley Road. Both routes join at a 90 bend in the road, from where the dominating tower of Robeston Wathen Church is clearly seen.

6. Follow the road north and across the ford (footbridge provided), then up the now very narrow sunken lane ("unsuitable for motors") up past an old spring house to the A40 at Robeston Wathen.

   Unfortunately a by-pass for Robeston Wathen is planned which will cut across this section of the walk. One can only hope that the damage to this ancient route is limited.

   Turn right, then cross over and take Church Lane past the foot of the Church tower (note the sundial) and on for three quarters of a mile past Abystree, a collection of cottages, where the road surface is lost and the route becomes a rough track, to a ford.

7. If the ford is impassable and the ancient sunken lane the other side flooded, you can by-pass both by turning right over a stile just before the ford and going parallel to the lane over a footbridge

and through fields back to Llawhaden Bridge, though if dry, the lane is very pleasant to walk.

Once back at Llawhaden Bridge cross the river and turn right, retracing the first part of the route past the Church and Castle to the car park and picnic site or turn left and follow the road to where it goes sharp left. Here go straight on up a sunken green lane, locally known as "Rock Hill". This leads you back up to the start of the walk through part of the Mediaeval village, traces of which in the form of house platforms can be found on either side of the sunken lane.

29: Narberth and Mounton Chapel

Distance: 7 miles (11km)

Time: 3-4 hours

Maps: OS Landranger 158 Tenby; OS Pathfinder 1080 Narberth; OS Outdoor Leisure 36 South Pembrokeshire

Start: Landsker Visitor Centre, Narberth OS 109 146

Parking: Large car park 108 147 signed in town

Terrain: Mainly excellent tracks and green lanes. Muddy in places. A little overgrown in one lane, but passable.

Nearest town: Narberth

Refreshments: Cafés, shops and pubs in Narberth

Stiles: 7

Suitable for: All. Dogs on leads across farmland.

Along the way

Narberth is a fascinating little town and its history is well recorded in the Landsker Visitor Centre. The ruins of the Norman Castle (worth looking at, but not on route) are probably on the site of the Court of Pwyll mentioned in the Welsh legends of "The Mabinogion", and Narberth was once the capital of the Kingdom of Dyfed.

Once a centre for cattle droving and scene of the Rebecca Riots, Narberth was on the Landsker, or border, between the English and Welsh-speaking parts of Pembrokeshire, but now makes an excellent centre from which to explore both parts of the county.

Mounton Chapel, visited on the walk, was once well-used despite its isolation, and dates from the 13th century, though heavily restored in the 18th and 19th centuries. Sadly it is now in a dangerously ruinous state and should not be entered, though it makes a romantic and mysterious place for a lunch stop.

Green Lane near point 3

The Walk

1. Leave the Visitor Centre and head south-east to the war memorial cross where you turn left. Follow the road for about 100 metres then turn right up a narrow road by two trees and follow the road along the side of the United Reform Church. This road skirts a housing development and soon peters out into a grass track.

2. At the T-junction of tracks, turn right over a way-marked stile and follow the right-hand hedge of the fields over two stiles, then left over a third stile and right again along the right-hand hedge to a gateway.

   Go through the gateway and follow the left-hand hedge to a gate and stile into a narrow lane. Follow this lane for about 200 metres, crossing a bridge to a T-junction where you come to a tarmac farm drive.

3. Turn left, then leave the tarmac after 100 metres, turning diagonally left again along a way-marked track into the trees.

   After about 400 metres you come to a major track junction and turn right, almost doubling back at first, into a sunken lane signposted as a cycle route. This track improves as you climb past a farm and some cottages to a quiet road.

4. Cross the road into a continuation of the track opposite and follow this for 900 metres up to the A478. Cross the road and turn left, then right after 100 metres, up a farm drive. Continue past the farm on a green lane to a major track junction where you turn right and continue to a second junction 200 metres further on.

5. Turn left here, ignoring the way-marks for the Knights Way that goes straight on, and follow the track into a farmyard. Turn right and go down the farm drive for 200 metres, then turn left up a steep-sided lane between two telegraph pole gate-posts, found just before a dogleg bend in the farm drive.

   Fairly clear to start with, this sunken lane passes a ruined cottage and then becomes more overgrown – though passable – until you duck under a fence (no stile) into a farmyard.

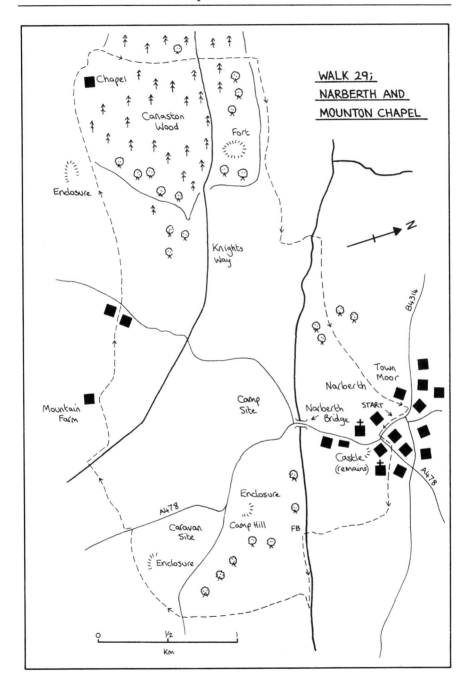

WALK 29;
NARBERTH AND
MOUNTON CHAPEL

Chapel

Canaston Wood

Fort

Enclosure

Knights Way

Mountain Farm

Camp Site

Narberth

Town Moor

Narberth Bridge

START

Castle (remains)

Enclosure

Caravan Site

Camp Hill

FB

Enclosure

Enclosure

B4314

A478

A478

0   ½
Km

6. Go straight on through the farmyard to the road, cross directly over and into a continuation of the track, now well used as a farm drive, and follow this for about 450 metres.

   Where the drive swings left, go straight on through a gate until the main track again swings left where you again go straight on over a gate.

   Follow the right-hand hedge until you find yourself in a hedged green lane, then (as much as possible) the left-hand hedge as a field opens up on the right, and cross a fence (again no stile but an easy crossing) in the top corner of the field into a large field above the woods.

   Follow the right-hand fence, above the woods, as you cross the field, then skirt a muddy area of trees and springs, keeping up to the left of any problems until you see Mounton Chapel.

7. After admiring this picturesque ruin, cross the stile in the boundary above the porch end of the chapel and turn right into an ancient sunken – and often wet – lane.

   Follow this for 150 metres to a way-marked track junction where the route goes right into Canaston Woods and leaves the stream.

   Keep to this path for the full three-quarters of a mile across the wood, ignoring many side turnings. Partway through the wood the path crosses a major track, a continuation of the Knights Way seen earlier, before dropping down and out of the wood to reach the tarmac Valley Road.

8. Turn right and follow the quiet road for about 1 mile to a turning to the left way-marked and signed "Shipping Factory". Take this turn and descend to a way-marked fork in the track where you go left, cross a concrete bridge over a stream and follow the well-surfaced and charmingly-named "Carding Mill Lane", an ancient green lane, back up to Narberth.

9. The path comes out via parkland to the car park and up to the road where you turn right and right again to come back to the Landsker Visitor Centre.

30: Marloes and St Brides

Distance: 9½ miles (15.5km)

Time: 4-5 hours

Maps: OS Landranger 157 St David's & Haverfordwest; OS Pathfinder Sheets 1102 Skomer Island and 1079 Haverfordwest; OS Outdoor Leisure 36 South Pembrokeshire

Start: 779081 Marloes Sands Car Park

Terrain: Good. Coast Path with few ascents or descents, and good field paths and tracks.

Nearest town: Haverfordwest

Parking: See Start

Refreshments: Lobster Pot Inn, Marloes, highly recommended for both food and drink.

Stiles: 29 – all in good condition.

Suitable for: All. Keep dogs on leads in most places. Keep children under control on the Coast Path as the cliffs are close, sheer and, in places, crumbling.

Along the way

This walk, a mixture of easy Coast Path and inland walking, takes in beautiful cliff scenery and can also offer sandy beaches for prolonged breaks on the way.

Most of the Marloes peninsula is owned by the National Trust. At Martin's Haven you will find boat trips to Skomer Island Nature Reserve, which is highly recommended (no dogs allowed on Skomer), as well as other island trips. The whole area around Skomer and the Deer Park is a Marine Nature Reserve and many divers will be seen in Martin's Haven preparing to explore this area.

St Brides, now only boasting a small Celtic-style church dedicated

Deadman's Bay and the Deer Park

to St Bridget, and a few other buildings, was once an important settlement with the whole bay from Skomer to St David's being named after it.

On the way flora and fauna abound. Keep your eyes open for pinks, gorse, violets, bladder campion, bluebells, primroses in the spring, other seasonal flowers, signs of badgers, seals, dolphins, all sorts of sea birds and more.

The Walk

1. From the car park entrance turn down the un-surfaced lane past the Youth Hostel. 300 metres past this, turn left on a path – not marked on the Landranger map – signposted across fields to the Coast Path.

2. Turn right on the Coast Path and follow this past Gate-Holm Island (Gate Holm is Norse for Goat Island) which boasts an ancient settlement with remains of over 100 rectangular huts,

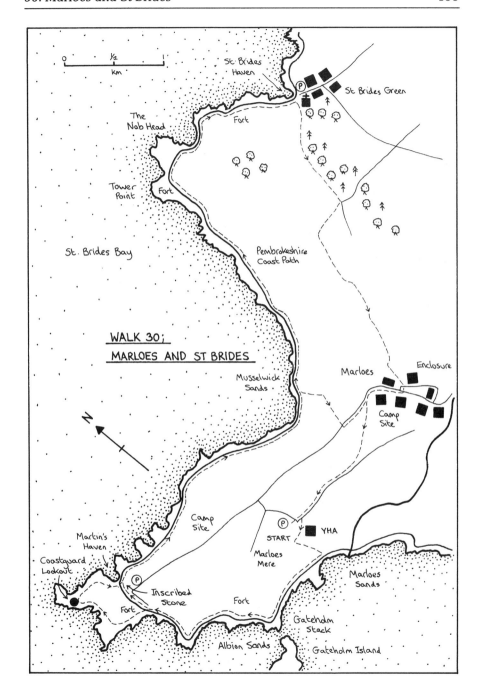

0   ½
km

St Brides
Haven

St Brides Green

The
Nob Head

Fort

Tower
Point   Fort

St. Brides Bay

Pembrokeshire
Coast Path

WALK 30;
MARLOES AND ST BRIDES

Musselwick
Sands

Marloes   Enclosure

N

Camp
Site

Camp
Site

Martin's
Haven

Coastguard
Lookout

P

Inscribed
Stone

P

START

Marloes
Mere

P   YHA

Marloes
Sands

Fort

Fort

Gateholm
Stack

Albion Sands   Gateholm Island

and on through the banks of an ancient fort along cliffs giving views of Skokholm Island.

3. The craggy cliffs and rocky coves are not only excellent scenic value but are also interesting to geologists, while part of the wreck of the Albion which came to grief around 1840, can be seen at low tide by Gate Holm Sound. This is a Site of Special Scientific Interest.

4. Crossing the stile into the walled Deer Park, you have the choice of following the cliffs around this section, or dropping down right by the wall in a short cut to Martin's Haven. There is no evidence of deer ever having been kept in the Deer Park.

5. Martin's Haven has toilets, a display on the Nature Reserves and a 7-9th century stone with a carved ring cross that probably marked a Celtic burial or prayer station. The stone was unearthed during National Trust works in the area in some time around 1982.

   Leaving Martin's Haven by steep steps, you regain the cliff path which takes you past Musselwick Sands.

6. Reached by steps cut into the living rocks, this almost-always empty beach offers an expanse of sand at low tide, but only curiously-shaped rocks at high tide. It is always a good spot for lunch.

   There is the option of a short-cut back to the start from here if time is pressing.

7. Continuing past Nabs Head with its blow hole, mesolithic stone working floor and Iron Age fort, you follow a stone wall over which you can see the former family seat of the Barony of Kensington on your right as you descend to St Brides Haven.

8. Go through the churchyard and out through the iron gate opposite the church door, and cross the drive following the wall on your left along a well way-marked path.

   Cross a track and follow the path across several fields, sticking to the left boundaries until you reach a small lane.

   Turn right up this lane, then after 300 metres, turn left up a track alongside a field. At the top of the field where the track bears sharp right, turn left, cross a stile, then turn right and follow the right-hand boundary through several fields to an un-surfaced lane.

Follow the lane right for 200 metres, then take a field path to the left, keeping to the right-hand hedge, through the backyard of a house, and into Marloes village where you will find toilets, pubs and a shop.

9. Turn right along the road and follow this for about 400 metres through and out of the village, then take a field path to your left which brings you out on a road by Marloes Court Farm.

   Follow the road to the right and you will arrive back at the start of the walk.

10. On a sunny day a diversion down to Marloes Sands is recommended.

31: The Dale Peninsula

Distance: 7 miles (11.25km)

Time: 4 hours

Maps: OS Landranger 157 St David's & Haverfordwest area; Pathfinder Sheets 1102 Skomer Island and 1103 Milford Haven and Pembroke; OS Outdoor Leisure 36 South Pembrokeshire

Start: Car Park in centre of Dale 811 058

Terrain: Coast Path, field paths and a little road walking.

Nearest town: Haverfordwest

Parking: See Start, or half mile before Dale between the road and the sea.

Refreshments: Griffin Inn, Dale. Good food and drink in an inn of character on the sea front. The pub is said to be haunted by a dog and a woman.

Stiles: 22!

Suitable for: All. Dogs on leads. Keep children under control as the cliffs are high and in places unstable. Take care on the narrow roads in Dale. These can be busy in the season.

Along the way

The Dale peninsula shows how valuable this area has been in the past with many historical defences. These include the banks and ditches of an Iron Age fort on Great Castle Head, the ruins of Dale Castle, a Victorian fort (now a Field Centre) on Dale Point and another on West Blockhouse Point, as well as the remains of WWII emplacements scattered along the way – destroyed and now almost invisible.

On Watwick Point there is a large beacon and on West Blockhouse Point there are three transit marks, while St Ann's Head has a fully equipped Coastguard Station and an old, as well as current, light-

Mill Bay, on the Dale Peninsular

house, all of which reflect the importance of Milford Haven as a commercial waterway.

In 1485 Henry Tudor landed in narrow, rocky, Mill Bay on his way from Brittany to defeat Richard III at Bosworth Field. Why he chose to land in this seemingly dangerous rocky bay rather than the sands of Dale is a mystery to me.

This walk follows good paths around the peninsula and is well way-marked and maintained. Although the path can be muddy in places, the going is fairly gentle. Excellent views of Skokholm, Skomer and Grassholm Islands are to be had from the rugged Western Cliffs while views over Milford Haven and South Pembrokeshire dominate the Eastern half of the walk. In rough weather the cliffs with breaking waves are truly dramatic.

The Walk

1. Leave the car park in the centre of Dale and turn left along the sea front for 100 metres. Take the first turn to your left and follow the road up past the church on your left.

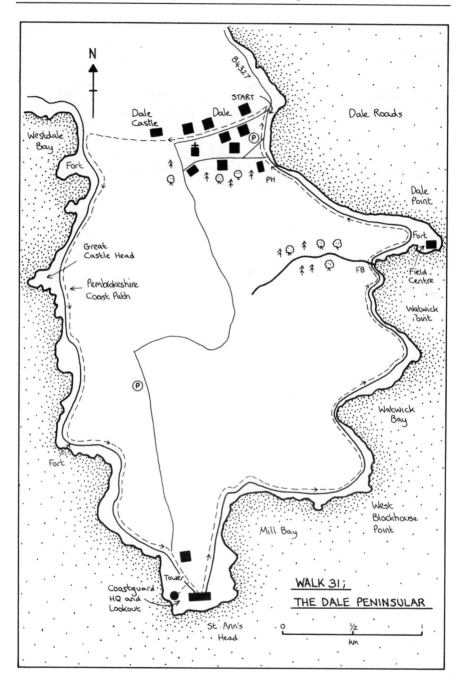

N

START

B4327

Dale Roads

Dale Castle

Dale

Westdale Bay

Fort

Dale Point

PH

Great Castle Head

Fort

Field Centre

Pembrokeshire Coast Path

FB

Watwick Point

P

Watwick Bay

Fort

West Blockhouse Point

Mill Bay

Tower

Coastguard HQ and Lookout

WALK 31;
THE DALE PENINSULAR

St Ann's Head

0   ½   1

km

2. When the road goes sharp left, go straight on through a gate ahead and up a farm track under the ruins of Dale Castle (private). When the track turns left after 100 metres, go straight on over a stile and follow a field path past ponds to the cliffs above Westdale Bay.

3. Turn left and climb the steps up to the fort on Great Castle Head and follow the mainly level path past cliff slumps and past the National Trust properly of Kete, by rugged cliff scenery to St Ann's Head and the Coastguard station and lighthouse.

4. Follow the well-signed path past the buildings with perhaps a short (signposted) diversion to the viewpoint at "Cobblers Hole".

5. After leaving the buildings, the path descends to Mill Bay – scene of Henry Tudor's landing in 1485 – before climbing back onto the cliffs.

The undulating path is very straight-forward and continues past West Blockhouse Point and round Watwick Bay before descending through woods to Castle Beach Bay and climbing up to the lane that services Dale Fort Field Centre.

6. Turn left on the lane and follow it back through woodland to the start in Dale, with its yachts, dinghies and sailboards.

32: Landshipping and Cresswell Quay

Distance: 12½ miles (20km)

Time: 6 hours

Maps: OS Landranger 158 Tenby; OS Pathfinder 1104 Tenby and Saundersfoot and 1080 Narberth; OS Outdoor Leisure 36 South Pembrokeshire

Start: Stanley Arms, Landshipping (013116)

Terrain: Easy walking on mainly well way-marked paths, lanes and shoreline. Muddy in places.

Nearest Towns: Narberth, Pembroke, Haverfordwest.

Parking: Roadside parking near pub at start.

Refreshments: Pubs at Landshipping, Lawrenny Quay and Cresswell Quay. Tea Rooms at Lawrenny (limited summer opening).

Stiles: 25 (less if high tide alternatives are used)

Suitable for: All. Dogs on leads through farm land.

Along the way

This walk takes in quiet lanes, woodland and field paths and tidal foreshore, as well as small villages that look as if they have slept since the dawn of time. However, this now quiet area was once a hive of activity with coal from the Pembrokeshire Coal Field and limestone being loaded onto ships at Landshipping, Cresswell and Lawrenny Quays, and ship-building being carried out at Lawrenny where, during WWII, there was a RN sea plane base.

These days pleasure craft use the Quays, walkers and farmers the land, and peace and quiet rule. The roads are quiet even in high summer and the walking is most enjoyable.

The church and viewpoint at Lawrenny are both well worth a

Garron Pill

visit, the church for its historical connections, the viewpoint for the best view of the day.

The Walk

From the Stanley Arms at the start of the walk, follow the road north-west, then south where views over the fields to the junction of the Eastern and Western Cleddau are to be seen, down to Landshipping Quay.

1. From here you have a choice. If the tide is out, follow the strand line path alongside the water where overhanging trees have their branches festooned with seaweed, for 1¼ miles to where the path cuts up through Sams Wood (a missing way-mark after a quarter of a mile can cause confusion at one junction, but go up a steep path with a wooden handrail visible further up the bank), then across fields and up a lane to Coedcanlas Farm, where Dick Francis, the author, lived.

    If the tide is in, follow the signposted High Tide alternative from

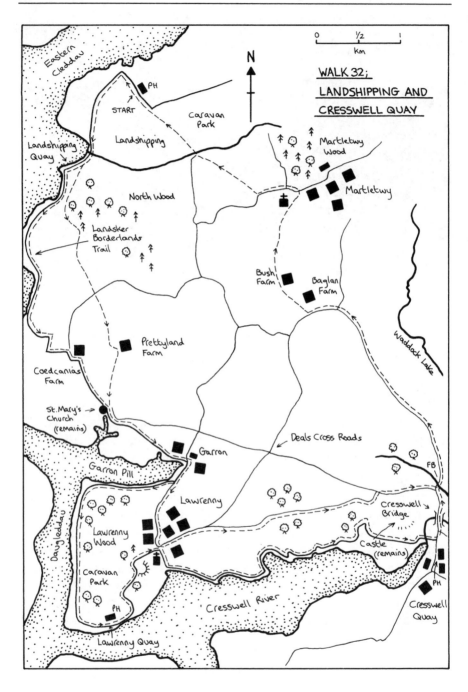

WALK 32;
LANDSHIPPING AND
CRESSWELL QUAY

Landshipping Quay which takes you up a lane, through a rather muddy wood and across fields to Prettyland Farm, and then by quiet lane to rejoin the main path where it meets the tarmac beyond Coedcanlas Farm.

2. From here the well way-marked path crosses farmland above "Beggars Reach" to the road at Garron Pill where at high tide the road may be flooded, but a raised footpath with footbridges helps keep you dry shod.

3. Turn right along the road and if the tide is in, follow the road up to Lawrenny village with its ancient church.

   If the tide is out, follow the strand line along Garron Pill for half a mile before leaving the water's edge for a woodland stroll with views over the estuary to Benton Castle, round to Lawrenny Quay.

   Just past the Lawrenny Arms Hotel, the path follows a track into the woods and up to a picnic site and viewpoint where Lawrenny Castle once stood (a Victorian mansion) before descending to the church in Lawrenny village.

4. From the church entrance you have (again) a choice. At low tide turn right, following the signs for Lawrenny Quay and at the foot of a short hill, take the well way-marked path through fields and woods that follows the side of the Cresswell River (occasionally meandering inland) and eventually down through Scotland Wood to rudimentary stepping stones – not needed at very low tide when you can cross almost dry shod – to Cresswell Quay). Turn left and follow the quiet country lanes signposted to Martletwy.

5. At high tide, cross the road outside the church and take the quiet road through the village of Lawrenny signposted to Cresswell and join the main route just north of Cresswell Quay. Turn left or drop down to Cresswell Quay for a pleasant diversion.

6. After following the road from Cresswell Quay northwards for 2 miles, turn left at a junction signed to Lawrenny and follow this for 500 metres before turning up a way-marked farm track through Baglan Farm to Bush Farm. Here the way-marks lead

you through the farmyard and onto a green track that takes you down across fields to a muddy ford. To the right of this impassable ford a stile leads you into the woods where the path crosses two streams before taking you through fields and someone's back garden to the road by the church in Martletwy.

7. Turn left and follow the road for 400 metres where you turn right up a green lane. The way-marked path then leads you across fields and down to a road. Turn right over the bridge and go straight up the road for 1 mile back to the start of the walk.

```
┌─────────────────────────────────────────────┐
│ ┌─────────────────────────────────────────┐ │
│ │                                         │ │
│ │    33: Walking around Angle             │ │
│ │                                         │ │
│ └─────────────────────────────────────────┘ │
└─────────────────────────────────────────────┘
```

Distance: 9½ miles (15km)

Time: 5 hours

Maps: OS Landranger 157 St David's & Haverfordwest; OS Pathfinder 1103 Milford Haven; OS Outdoor Leisure 36 South Pembrokeshire

Start: Centre of Angle, 864029

Terrain: Mainly good coast paths. Some steep ascents and descents. Some road walking on quiet lanes

Nearest town: Pembroke

Parking: At start by Hibernia Inn or at West Angle Bay 853031

Refreshments: Café at West Angle Bay and Hibernia Inn, Angle

Stiles: 37

Suitable for: Most people. Keep dogs on leads over farmland and where signed. Children should be kept under control as the cliffs are often close, sheer and loose.

Along the way

The area around Angle is one of the quietest parts of the Pembrokeshire National Park and offers superb walking with plenty of interest along the way.

Although the waterway of Milford Haven is dominated by oil refineries and a power station, these rarely intrude even when visible, while the importance of the Haven is emphasised by the many ruins of fortifications, ancient, Victorian and more modern, that are passed on the way.

Angle itself holds the remains of a fortified tower house, a ruined dovecote and a charming church with separate seaman's chapel and a Norman iron-bound wooden font.

Keep your eyes open for a wide variety of birds, including choughs and sparrowhawks.

Loking west from Freshwater Bay

The Walk

1. From the centre of the sleepy village head east past the church and onto a private road, signposted the Coastal Path, that leads you along the waterfront on a good tarmacadam surface.

2. When this road swings inland continue along the foreshore for 150 metres to where a public road comes down to the shore. Turn right and follow this quiet road up through charming pheasant-filled woods to the main (but quiet) road. Turn left, then, almost opposite the track to Hardings Hill Farm, go through the second gate on your right. Follow the way-marked path down the right side of one field, across the middle of a second field and across a sometimes boggy stream valley. Turn right along the rim of this valley to gain the Coast Path by Gravel Bay.

3. The view across Freshwater West Bay to Castlemartin Ranges is stunning and this bay – noted for its empty golden sands – exposes an ancient drowned forest at low tide.

   Turn right away from the bay and follow the Coast Path which soon gives stiff walking as it plunges up and down several steep

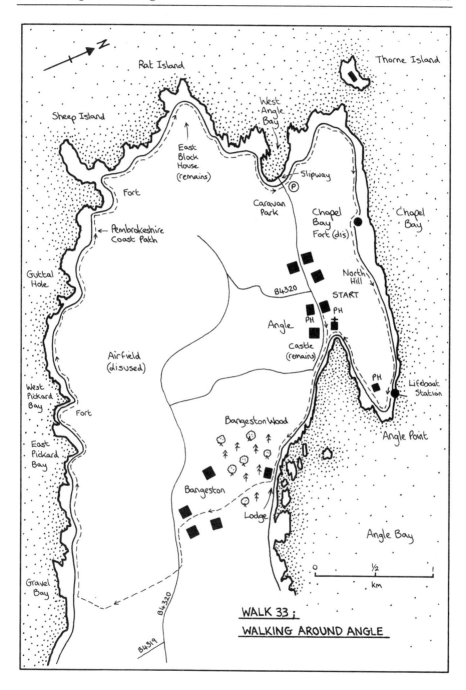

WALK 33 ;
WALKING AROUND ANGLE

stream valleys. In places the path has been realigned, so follow the obvious way-marking.

4. Note the remains of an Iron Age Fort between East and West Pickard Bays.

5. After Guttle Hole – a stupendous cliff formation – the walking becomes easier, but still offers good views as you pass Sheep Island with its Iron Age and 1st World War defences and lookout.

6. As you approach Rat Island, the MOD radio station dominates the view, though as you pass *between* signs saying "MOD Property Keep Out" it is obvious from remains of WWI, WWII and Victorian defences that this has always been an important military site. Indeed, the remains of the East Block House are post-Armada defences.

   The obvious way-marking leads you safely through MOD land with excellent views across Milford Haven to St Ann's Head where Henry VII landed in 1485 on his way to win his crown at Bosworth Field, and down past an ancient burial ground to the café and toilets at West Angle Bay.

7. From West Angle Bay you can cut the walk short and return to Angle along the road, or continue up the far side of the bay past the ruined lime kilns and onto the cliffs that dominate Milford Haven.

8. Thorn Island was once a Victorian fort, but is now an hotel, while at various points along this section, massive defences and batteries are now almost lost in trees and undergrowth below the path.

9. Dropping down alongside fields on North Hill where mediaeval strip fields survive in the present pattern, the path crosses the access road to the present lifeboat station and above the ruins of the old one, before reaching the foreshore by the Old Point House pub, a 15th century building with superb views.

10. Follow the foreshore track back to Angle, and the start of the walk.

34: Bosherston and Barafundle

Distance: 9 miles or 8 miles (14.5km or 13km)

Time: 5 hours (longer if you decide on a swim)

Maps: OS Landranger 158 Tenby; OS Pathfinder 1124 Castlemartin and St Govan's Head; OS Outdoor Leisure 36 South Pembrokeshire

Start: Bosherston car park 966 948

Terrain: Good paths, woodland, lakeshore, beaches, cliff path and quiet lanes.

Nearest town: Pembroke

Parking: See Start

Refreshments: Olde Worlde café and St Govan's Inn and shop at Bosherston. Armstrong Arms, Stackpole. National Trust tearooms Stackpole Quay. Ice cream vans at most car parks on route in the season.

Stiles: 4-6

Suitable for: Children, and dogs on leads.

Along the way

This walk starts by skirting the edge of the famous Bosherston lily ponds, limestone valleys flooded in the 18th century by the Stackpole Estate, and which form the largest area of fresh water in Pembrokeshire. Although attractive all year round, these are best seen in June when the lilies are in full bloom.

Further on, and ideal for family bathing, is Barafundle Beach, possibly the best and most attractive bay in Pembrokeshire.

Broadhaven also offers good bathing, while if the path across the MOD Ranges is open (no red flags flying), the longer version of the walk takes you to St Govan's Chapel. This little-restored 11th or 13th century chapel nestles in a narrow rocky gorge in the cliffs on the

Stackpole Quay

site of a 5th century hermit's cell and is reached by steep stone steps. The chapel is linked with St Govan and Arthurian legend.

The majority of this walk passes through the National Trust's Stackpole Estate and there are excellent information panels at various points.

The cliffs all offer stunning views. The bird life along the walk is very varied, from the extensive range of sea birds nesting on the cliffs to kingfishers and woodpeckers in the woods by the lakes. Seals and occasional dolphins can be seen off-shore.

The Walk

1. Leave the car park by the grassy path along its southern (right hand) edge past an interpretation board, and down steps toward the lily ponds. At the bottom of the steps take the path to the left signposted "Broad Haven 1 m" and cross the pond on a causeway bridge. Follow the well-marked trail under the flank of an Iron Age fort across another arm of the ponds on a second narrow

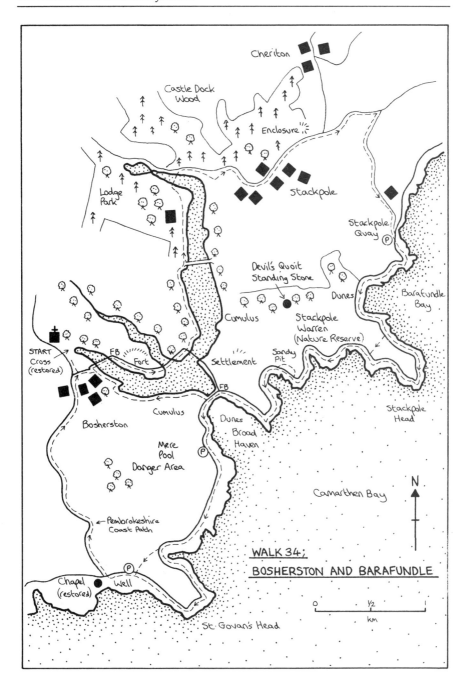

Cheriton

Castle Dock
Wood

Enclosure

Lodge
Park

Stackpole

Stackpole
Quay

Devil's Quoit
Standing Stone

Dunes

Barafundle
Bay

Cumulus

Stackpole
Warren
(Nature Reserve)

START
Cross
(restored)

FB

Fort

Settlement

Sandy
Pit

FB

Stackpole
Head

Cumulus

Bosherston

Dunes

Broad
Haven

Mere
Pool
Danger Area

Camarthen Bay

N

← Pembrokeshire
Coast Path

Chapel
(restored)

Well

WALK 34;
BOSHERSTON AND BARAFUNDLE

St. Govan's Head

0   ½   1
km

bridge and up to a track. Turn right (signposted "Broad Haven") and descend to "Green Bridge" or as it is also known "Grassy Bridge".

2. Do not cross the bridge, but turn left up a path signposted "Eastern Arm" and follow this alongside the water through mixed deciduous woods, under a cliff hung bank, and past the attractive "8 Arch Bridge".

3. Again, do not cross the bridge, but follow the path signposted "permissive path Stackpole Court Site" along the waterside and past an old boat-house, now a wheelchair-accessible bird hide.

   Follow the handrailed path and on reaching the buildings, turn right through an archway, then left up stone steps to a grass terrace which you cross to a small car park and interpretation board in the far corner.

   This terrace was the site of the former Stackpole Court and there is a small information display, explaining the history of the house and lake, in the former Game Larder.

4. From this car park ignore the main track and take a small way-marked path, by the lockable barrier, that drops down from the north-east corner into the woods. This brings you to the "Hidden Bridge" and spillover weir.

   To someone standing on the One Arch Bridge, to your left, anyone crossing the Hidden Bridge appears to be walking on water.

   Follow this path until you come to a branching board-walked path off to the right just before a limestone "grotto" and arch. Follow this through the wet wood lane then go left on a ride and on to the quiet road to Stackpole.

5. Turn right and follow the road through the village past a T-junction keeping straight on to a second T-junction where the route turns right down a lane signposted "Stackpole Quay and Barafundle".

   This lane leads down past some National Trust holiday cottages and past an unusual square limekiln, then up again to where the coast path can be joined through holes in the low wall at the top of the slope.

6. Turn right and descend steps to Stackpole Quay, once the smallest harbour in Britain and built to import coal and export limestone from the nearby quarry (now a recreation ground). At the bottom of the steps you will find a National Trust tearoom and toilets.

   The route then climbs up more steps, following signs for Barafundle across the level cliff top and then through an archway in the old estate deer park wall to descend (more steps) to the delights of Barafundle Beach.

7. Cross – or linger on – this beach and take the steps up into the woods on the far side, climbing up to the cliff top path. At the stile you have a choice of following the cliff edge round Stackpole Head by taking the left of two paths, or cutting across the neck of the headland by taking the right-hand path.

   The paths rejoin on the south of the head and follow way-marks around the impressive cliffs, riddled with caves and sink holes and which are covered with nesting birds in the season, round Saddle Point to Broadhaven.

8. Here you have choices – bathe, build sand castles, return to the start by going inland by the west side of the lily ponds, or continuing across the beach and across the Ranges to St Govan's Chapel on a broad path clearly way-marked and flanked by warnings about keeping to the path. The latter option is only viable when the MOD Ranges are not in use.

9. On reaching the car park at St Govan's, turn left by the far fence (on to further sections of the Ranges), and down the steep steps to find the charming chapel in its cleft in the rocks.

   After exploring, climb back up to the road which is followed back to Bosherston, St Michael's Church becoming a notable land-mark as you near the village.

35: A Circumnavigation of St David's

Distance: 20-24 miles (32-39km)

Time: 10 hours

Maps: OS Pathfinder 1055 St David's and Solva, OS Landranger 157 St David's and Haverfordwest area, OS Outdoor Leisure 35 North Pembrokeshire

Start/Finish: Whitesands Bay Car Park 734271

Refreshments: Whitesands Bay car park (seasonal). Possibility of refreshments vans at various points in season.

Parking: See Start

Terrain: Coastal path – many ups and downs – farmland – some stiff climbs – easy scrambles on Carn Penbiri and Carn Llidi

Nearest town: St David's

Suitable for: The very fit!

Along the way

The St David's peninsula features some of the best coast walking in Britain. There are soaring cliffs, deep inlets and sandy beaches, all topped by well-maintained footpaths. This circular walk joins two ends of the coastal horseshoe around the peninsula with a rural walk along, or near, the "Ffos y Mynach", or Monks Dyke.

This route follows an ancient boundary reputed to mark the limits of the religious lands of St David's. Monks were not allowed outside the dyke, while inside was held to have special rights of sanctuary. The Ffos y Mynach is mainly a green path between high hedges planted on top of walls in Pembroke style and contrasts with the open nature of the cliff path.

The walk is littered with sites of historical and prehistoric interest, the views are spectacular, especially from the summits of Carn Penbiri and Carn Llidi, and while the Coast Path has a few steep climbs and comes very close to the cliff edge at times, the paths are well-maintained and easy to walk, and are in the main well way-marked.

This can be done as a one day (strenuous) or two day (easier) walk. This area is noted for its wild flowers including orchids, flag iris, foxgloves, and wild life. Keep your eyes open for seals, dolphins, buzzards, a wide variety of sea birds from razorbills to cormorants, and inland, badgers and rabbits.

Looking south to St. David's Head

Day One

Leave the car park heading south in front of the surf rescue building and follow the obvious path past the site of a Roman station (two Roman roads and an ancient gold trade route from Ireland to Salisbury Plain finish at Whitesands) and follow the Coast Path round to St Justinian's where the ruins of a chapel on the site of a Celtic oratory can be seen, as well as the lifeboat house and slip featured in the BBC series "Lifeboat".

2. Continue southwards along the rugged coast with its views of Ramsey (R.S.P.B.) and its multitude of birds. Seals, dolphins and mad canoeists can be seen in these rough waters. Look for seal pups in the coves during the autumn. Ramsey (*Ramsey* being the Norse for 'Garlic Island') was once known as St David's Isle and holds a herd of red deer.

3. After ruins of an old mine at Penmaenmelyn, the coast turns eastwards and views of the coast change to the south and east across St Bride's Bay to Marloes peninsula and the beaches of Newgale and the Havens.

4. The path climbs and dips and eventually comes down to sea level at Porth Clais, the old port serving St David's and which features in Celtic legend. By the restored limekilns – used to burn limestone to produce lime for agricultural and building use – you may well find an ice-cream van in summer.

5. The path continues along the coast, climbing above cliffs that are favourites with rock climbers and wends its way into St Non's Bay where a detour into a field leads you to the ruins of St Non's Chapel. St Non was St David's mother and gave birth to him here during a storm. The nearby well sprang up at the same time and is reputed to have healing qualities. Try it on blisters and aching legs. The path past the well rejoins the Coast Path in front of the modern monastery.

6. The cliffs between Caerfai (another chance of an ice-cream van in the car park) and Caer Bwdy Bay were used to supply the Cathedral with building materials.

7. Three-quarters of a mile past the stream at Caer Bwdy, above a deep and craggy inlet, Ogof y Ffos (mis-spelt "Flos" on the 1:25,000 map), a faint path leaves the Coast Path and leads up to a just visible ladder stile. This is the southern end of the Ffos y Mynach which is confirmed by a finger post under the stile.

8. Follow this way-marked path northwards through fields, keeping the hedge bank on your left and onto a narrow lane. This leads to the main road, the A487, to St David's.

9. If you are taking two days for the walk, leave here to find

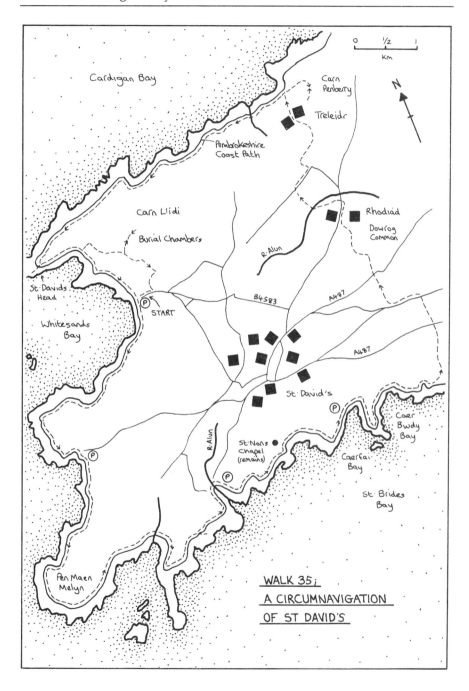

WALK 35;

A CIRCUMNAVIGATION

OF ST DAVID'S

overnight accommodation in St David's. There are occasional buses on this road, though the City centre is an easy 1¾ miles away.

Day Two

10. On regaining the point you left the previous night, cross the A487 (busy in the summer) and follow a green lane which runs for a quarter of a mile up to a narrow tarmac road.

11. Turn left here and follow this road on the course of a Roman road for half a mile down to Dwr Cleifion (water of the sick – more healing waters?) where you turn right, leaving the road for another green lane. Follow this northwards past where the stream has been dammed to form an irrigation pool and across the A487 (again) which here follows an old pilgrim route, and up to Dowrog Pool.

12. The Ffos y Mynach actually crosses this marsh – you can see the remains of the raised causeway – but unless you are suicidal, follow the way-marked diversion around to the west regaining the route near Caer Dewi (David's Stone). If the whole walk is being tackled in one day, this spot with its profusion of wild flowers makes a good place for lunch.

13. On reaching the road at Rhodiad Brenin, you leave the ancient route – it is no longer a right of way – turn right and follow the road turning left up a way-marked track just after crossing the bridge. Follow this track westward until you cross a small stream by way of a stone slab bridge, then bear north along the way-marked and somewhat boggy track. You are now on National Trust land and the worst of the boggy sections are board-walk covered.

14. On reaching the road, turn right (from here to Penberi the Ffos y Mynach is either totally blocked and/or not a right of way) then after a quarter of a mile turn left. Leave the road after 150 metres, turning right onto another ancient track, Feidr Dwr (Watery Lane) that can be wet.

15. When this reaches the road, turn left up to Treleidr, where a way-marked path climbs straight from the farmyard to join the Coast Path again below Carn Penbiri. A diversion to the top of Penbiri is recommended.

16. From here follow the Coast Path south-west. Navigation is easy, keeping to the obvious path bordering the cliffs, but beware of steep descents and proximity to lethal cliffs.

17. Below Carn Llidi note the traces of Iron Age settlements and fields in the valley to your left. 200 metres or so before you reach the Fort of St David's Head (with eight hut circles visible) there is a Neolithic burial chamber set between rock outcrops on your left.

18. From here follow the path east then south back to Whitesands Bay car park and your start point, or you can follow obvious paths up to the top of Carn Llidi (an easy scramble) past remains of wartime hydrophone and radar stations as well as Neolithic burial chambers.

A pleasant end to the day is made by swimming, or at least soaking your feet, in the sea here before stopping at the (seasonal) shop for an ice cream or cup of tea.

36: Walk back in time – a two-day trek over the Preseli Mountains

Distance: 18½ miles (30km)

Time: 10 hours

Maps: OS Landranger 145 Cardigan and surrounding area, OS Pathfinder 1033 Newport (Trefdraeth) and Eglwyswrw, OS Outdoor Leisure 35 North Pembrokeshire

Nearest town: Cardigan

Start: Roadside at map reference 165 330

Terrain: Hill walking and valley paths. Muddy in places.

Parking: Limited roadside parking at start

Suitable for: The very fit!

Note: All sections of this walk not on Rights of Way are by permission of the Barony of Kemes. Please do nothing to abuse this permission or it may be withdrawn in future. All dogs on leads please.

The walk starts at the eastern end of the Preseli Ridge, descends to Rosebush for an overnight stop before plunging down into Cwm Gwaun and ascending Mynydd Carn Ingli to finish in the charming seaside village of Newport.

Day One

1. Leaving your car on the roadside verge by Mountain Bach Farm 1½ miles from Crymych village on the Mynachlog-ddu road, a short stroll up a track brings you out onto the open hill where Foel Drygarn, an ancient volcano and your first objective, is clear to see.

2. A clear path climbs this hill, an Iron Age hill fort that is named

after the three Bronze Age cairns on its summit. Standing on these, you get a view of the walk ahead of you, the sea shimmering to the west and, on a clear day, the hills of Snowdonia and of the Brecon Beacons National Park can be seen in the distance.

Dropping down from this lofty viewpoint, you cross the still visible ramparts or weave through the craggy defences to pick up thin paths that take you southwards onto a broad, sometimes muddy, trail that you can then follow west towards the obvious rocky outcrops.

3. The broad trail is an ancient route with over 3,500 years of use. Once a trading route for Irish Celtic gold used by Romans, drovers and King Arthur, it will be followed for the majority of the day, while in the crags ahead is Carn Menyn where the Dolerite "Bluestones" of Stonehenge were quarried.

Just past here, the path dips into a saddle which can be quite boggy, and it is advisable to keep a little north, following the line of small curiously-shaped outcrops of rock, reminiscent of Dartmoor, as you head towards Carn Bica.

4. Before you reach this craggy top with its Bronze Age cairn, you join an old peat-cutting trail coming from the north which has ascended by the side of Carn Alw. This is another ancient hill fort, which also has connection with more modern conflict, being the place where the BBC filmed "Tumbledown", part of the story of the Falklands War.

5. More ancient remains in the form of a stone circle called "Bedd Arthur", or "Arthur's Grave" are found below Carn Bica, while wrecks of two WWII aircraft can be discovered in the area.

Dropping down to the west the path crosses a pass with another ancient route which: to the south, leads to the standing stones and stone circle on Gors Fawr; to the north, passes Carn Alw, into the Nyfer Valley.

The outcrops on the ridge ahead are said to be Arthur's knights turned to stone, and these are passed by the path as you climb up to Foel Feddau, with its prehistoric cairned summit before crossing the almost trackless moor in a south-westerly direction

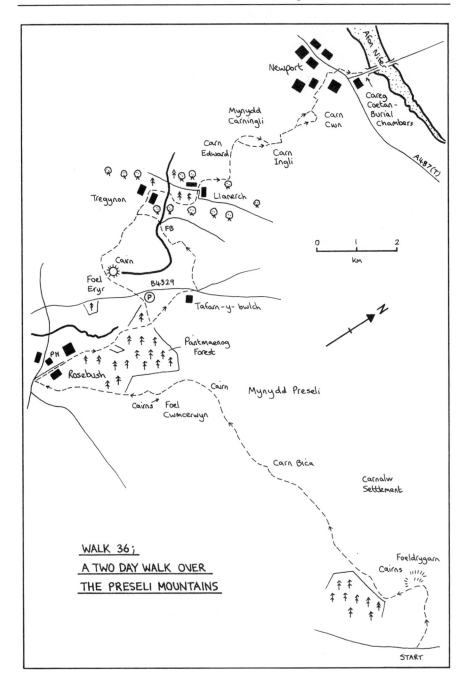

WALK 36;
A TWO DAY WALK OVER
THE PRESELI MOUNTAINS

to again climb gently, this time onto the highest summit in West Wales, Foel Cwmcerwyn.

6. Standing on one of the several Bronze Age cairns around this top (where I have found traces of modern pagan ritual), you get a superb view of West Wales, while below you to the east there are the remains of slate mining in the site of the Preselis' last Ice Age glacier, and yet another ancient settlement.

    Descending to the south you soon pick up the old quarry track, boggy in places, but smothered in bilberries in the season, which will lead you down to the road and Rosebush, where you can find your night's lodging.

7. Rosebush itself was once a famous tourist attraction with day excursions being organised by the railway company which normally carried the slate from the large and imposing quarries. Now the quarries are silent, the railway gone and Rosebush a quiet backwater.

Day Two

The start of the second day's walking takes you north by the old quarry track, up through a conifer forest back to the ridge from where you have a choice of routes. Either:

8. Follow the track north, the old coach road, to Tafarn y Bwlch then on farm tracks to Gernos-Fach, Gernos Fawr and Gelli Fawr, passing standing stones by Waun Mawn and a charming stream valley to reach the road at Pont Gelli Fawr.

9. Or, turn left and follow the ridge west along the side of the forest, crossing Bwlch Gwnt to climb Foel Eryr with its Bronze Age cairn and brass view indicator, and drop down west across open moor to join the road by Ty Gwyn.

10. From the road head down the driveway of Trefynon where way-marks and a good path lead you down past an ancient homestead, complete with interpretation board, into the beautiful wooded valley of Cwm Gwaun. With many ancient sites on the rim of the valley plus rare lichens growing on the trees, the

Gwaun is a popular area for day visitors, but thanks to narrow roads and poor access, never gets too crowded.

11. This valley has an air of separateness and it is not surprising to learn that the inhabitants kept to the old Julian calendar long after the rest of Britain had switched to the Gregorian calendar.

12. Follow the clear path up the valley, north-east, until you come to a road, then cross to climb the far slopes through Llanerch Farm where peacocks and other exotic birds decorate the yard.

13. A good, if damp, track climbs steadily through the woods until you strike north-west up a narrow path to gain the open moor of Carn Ingli Common after passing the looming rocks of Carn Edward.

14. You can then either follow a broad track that curves north-east to reach Carn Ingli fort, another ex-volcano, or take narrow sheep trails past hut circles to Carn Briw, the summit of the moor, before turning east to gain the grand view of the rocky fort, and crossing the moor to gain this, your final top. At times this moor shows signs of extensive burning, but soon recovers to bloom with heather and gorse and to glow with rich colours.

15. Carn Ingli fort is another Iron Age hill fort, and its tumbled walls are clear to see. From the craggy summit you get dramatic views over Newport Bay and the craggy coastline which forms part of the Pembrokeshire Coast National trail, itself an excellent walk. The summit of Carn Ingli is where the Celtic Saint Brynach came to commune with angels and must have been a tough place to pray, but with a heavenly view. Once you leave the rocks of the top, the path to Newport drops northward in a clear grassy run, past more prehistoric remains that are not quite so obvious to the untrained eye.

Just before the open hillside is left behind via a gate for lanes leading down into Newport, turn off right to a small outcrop of rock, Carn Cwn, and you will find, in a split in the rocks, a "wishing well", reputedly tidal and quite unusual in appearance as the pool is trapped on a deep shelf and difficult to reach. It is cold and tastes beautifully pure.

16. Follow narrow lanes through to Newport's Kings Street, cross the

A487 following signs for the Golf Club and you will find a cromlech, Careg Coetan, hidden up on your left behind a small housing development. Not all the uprights support the massive cap stone, but this, the last prehistoric feature of the walk is, I trust, quite secure.

17. A few more metres down the road you come to a bridge over the Afon Nyfer and the coastal path, and the walk is over. You can now think about finding your bed for the night, a café, campsite, or pub, depending on time of day and inclination.

Newport caters for visitors quite well with plenty of accommodation and pubs, a few art galleries and souvenir shops and an interesting shore.

On the far side of the river, which can be waded at low tide, there are Newport Sands, while the town itself, with its castle, ancient limekilns, standing stones and other points of interest, can occupy half a day by itself. The modern world can be ignored on this walk as peace and quiet, plus relaxation and gentle exercise come to the fore.

Careg Coetan – see 17

A Welsh Language Primer

Visitors to Wales may be surprised to find Welsh being spoken as a first language, while place names may at first prove unpronounceable and incomprehensible. Do not fear – English is spoken by everyone and many road signs and place names are in both Welsh and English. To help with understanding some of the more common Welsh place names, here is a small selection of commonly used words and phrases, pronunciations and translations.

a   = ah
c   = k (hard)
ch = as in the Scottish "loch"
dd = th in "the"
e   = eh
f   = v
ff = f
g   = as in "go" (hard)
i   = ee
ll = almost a "th" sound.
       Say "l" and gently blow through tongue in this position
o   = oh
th = as in "through"
w   = often as "oo". Cwm (valley) sounds like "coomb"
y   = as e in "the" (y or yr), or as i. Dyffryn therefore sounds like "duffrin".

Some words commonly used in place names include:

aber	= estuary, river-mouth or confluence of streams
afon	= river
bach, fach	= small
bedd	= grave
betws	= chapel or oratory
blaen	= head of the valley
bont, pont	= bridge
braich	= arm
brith	= speckled
bryn	= hill

bwlch	=	pass, defile
bychan	=	little
cadair	=	chair
cae	=	field
caer	=	fort
capel	=	chapel
carn, carnedd	=	pile of stones
carreg	=	rock
castell	=	castle
cefn	=	ridge
celli, gelli	=	grove
clogwyn	=	precipice
coch	=	red
coed	=	woodland
cors, gors	=	bog
craig	=	rock
crib	=	narrow ridge
croes	=	cross
cwm	=	valley
dinas	=	fort
dol, ddol	=	meadow
drws	=	door
dwr	=	water
dyffryn	=	valley
eglwys	=	church
esgair	=	mountain shoulder
fawr, mawr	=	big
felin, melin	=	mill
ffordd	=	road
ffynnon	=	well, spring
foel, moel	=	rounded hill
fynydd, mynydd	=	mountain
gam	=	crooked
glan	=	bank, shore
glas, las	=	blue, green
glyder	=	head
glyn	=	glen
gwastad	=	plain, level ground
gwern	=	marsh
gwyn	=	white
gwynt	=	wind
hafod	=	summer dwelling
hen	=	old
hendre	=	winter dwelling
hir	=	long
isa, isaf	=	lower
llan	=	sacred enclosure, church
llethr	=	slope
llwyd	=	grey
llwyn	=	grove

llyn	=	lake
maen	=	stone
maes	=	field
morfa	=	coastal marsh
nant	=	brook, stream
newydd	=	new
ogof	=	cave
oleu	=	light
pant, bant	=	small hollow
pen	=	head, top
penrhyn	=	promontory
pentre, pentref	=	village
pistyll	=	spout, cataract
plas	=	mansion
pwll	=	pool
rhaeadr	=	waterfall
rhiw	=	hill
rhos	=	moorland, marsh
rhyd	=	ford
sarn	=	paved way, causeway
sych	=	dry
tan	=	under
tarren	=	hill
tir	=	land
traeth	=	stretch of shore
tre	=	town, hamlet
tri	=	three
trwyn	=	nose, promontory
twll	=	hole
ty	=	house
tyddyn	=	smallholding
ucha, uchaf	=	upper
waun	=	moor
y	=	the, of the
yn	=	in
ynys	=	island
ysgol	=	school, ladder
ystrad	=	valley floor, strath

Useful and polite phrases to learn are:

Bore da (bor-eh-da)	=	good morning
Diolch (dee-olch)	=	thank you
Dim diolch	=	no thank you

Confusion can arise from the mutations and other variations found in the spellings of some Welsh words. For example, the name of the hill "Foel Drygarn" can also be rendered as "Foeldrygarn", a single word.

Other titles of interest from:

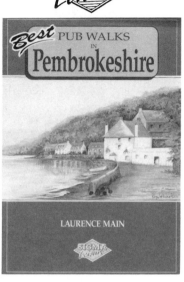

BEST PUB WALKS IN PEMBROKESHIRE

Laurence Main

If you enjoyed "Heritage Walks in Pembrokeshire", you're sure to appreciate this superb selection of walks based on welcoming Pembrokeshire pubs. Both inland and coastal walks are included and Laurence includes many local yarns – it's surprising how many pub regulars claim to have had supernatural experiences after imbibing the local ale!

(£6.95)

WALKS IN MYSTERIOUS WALES

Laurence Main

Follow the spirit paths of Wales - visit the most sacred and secret sites and discover ancient traditions of this historic country in the company of a leading expert. And, while you're discovering Welsh heritage, enjoy some excellent walks across the length and breadth of this ancient land.

(£6.95)

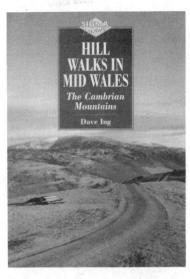

HILL WALKS IN MID WALES
The Cambrian Mountains

Dave Ing

This is one of the very few books to explore the pleasures of walking in Mid Wales - far from from the big mountains of Snowdonia and away from the crowds, yet so accessible for a day in the hills.

(£7.95)

SNOWDONIA ROCKY RAMBLES:
Geology beneath your feet

Bryan Lynas

Ten mountain walks that are voyages of discovery through time, with insights into the geology, wildlife and history of this rugged mountain region. This is the sequel to the author's highly-acclaimed "Lakeland Rocky Rambles" and has an introduction by James Lovelock FRS:
". . . a splendid guide . . . it opens the mind's eye to the form and structure of the land"

(£9.95)

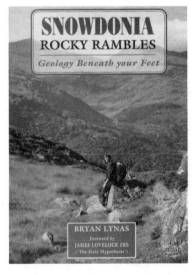

For further details or to obtain our complete catalogue, please contact:

Sigma Leisure, 1 South Oak Lane, Wilmslow, Cheshire SK9 6AR
Phone: 01625-531035; Fax: 01625-536800; E-mail: sigma.press@zetnet.co.uk
http://www.sigmapress.co.uk

ACCESS and VISA orders welcome – 24 hour Answerphone service! Most orders are despatched on the day we receive your order – you could be enjoying our books in just a couple of days. Please add £2 p&p to all orders.